Classroom in a Book

Adobe Acrobat version 3.0

D1511806

Library of Congress Catalog No.: 96-80332

ISBN: 1-56830-365-3

10 9 8 7 6 5 4 3 2 First Printing: April 1997

Published by Adobe Press, Adobe Systems Incorporated, San Jose, California. For information on becoming an Adobe Certified Expert (ACE) with Adobe Acrobat, send an e-mail to certification@adobe.com or visit the Adobe web site at (http://www.adobe.com).

The information in this book is furnished for informational use only, is subject to change without notice, and should not be construed as a commitment by Adobe Systems Incorporated. Adobe Systems Incorporated assumes no responsibility for any errors or inaccuracies that may appear in this book. The software mentioned in this book is furnished under license and may only be used or copied in accordance with the terms of such license.

Adobe, the Adobe Press logo, Adobe Type Manager, ATM, Acrobat, the Acrobat logo, Acrobat Capture, Acrobat Exchange, Acrobat Reader, Acrobat Catalog, Acrobat Distiller, PageMaker, FrameMaker, Illustrator, PostScript, and Classroom in a Book are trademarks of Adobe Systems Incorporated. America Online is a service mark of America Online, Inc. Apple, Macintosh, Power Macintosh, QuickTime, and TrueType are trademarks of Apple Computer, Inc. registered in the United States and other countries. CompuServe is a registered trademark of CompuServe Incorporated. Microsoft and Windows are either registered trademarks or trademarks of Microsoft Corporation in the United States and/or other countries. Macromedia Freehand is a trademark of Macromedia, Inc. Netscape and Netscape Navigator are trademarks of Netscape Communications Corporation. QuarkXPress is a registered trademark of Quark, Inc. UNIX is a registered trademark in the United States and other countries, licensed exclusively through X/Open Company, Ltd. Pentium is a trademark of Intel Corporation. All other brand or product names are the trademarks or registered trademarks of their respective holders.

Direct to plate pre-press and printing by GAC Shepard Poorman, Indianapolis, Indiana. Printed in the United States of America.

Published simultaneously in Canada.

Adobe Press books are published and distributed by Macmillan Computer Publishing USA. For individual, educational, corporate, or retail sales accounts, call 1-800-428-5331, or 317-581-3500. For information on Adobe Press books address Macmillan Computer Publishing USA, 201 West 103rd Street, Indianapolis, Indiana, 46290 or visit Macmillan's World Wide Web page (http://www.mcp.com/hayden/adobe).

Part number: 9000 6321 (4/97 MW)

Contents

Introduction

Prerequisites 1

About Classroom in a Book 1

System requirements 2

Adobe Acrobat Classroom in a Book
package contents 3

Getting started 4

Other resources 6

About Adobe products and services 6

**Introduction to Adobe
Acrobat Exchange 3.0**

Lesson 1

About Adobe Acrobat 10

Publishing PDF documents .11

Opening the work file 12

Looking at the work area 13

Navigating the document 13

Following a link 16

Retracing your viewing path 17

Using bookmarks and thumbnails 18

Watching a movie 20

Looking at a note 20

Searching for a word 21

Filling out a form 22

Review 24

Navigating and Linking   **Lesson 2**

About navigation 30

Opening the work file 31

About on-screen display 31

Navigating the magazine 33

Using and creating links 38

Review 48

Creating PDF   **Lesson 3**
Documents
Creating PDF documents 54

PDF Writer or Distiller? 54

Creating a PDF file with PDF Writer 55

Opening the work file 56

Using PDF Writer 56

Viewing the PDF file 58

Creating PDF with Distiller 59

Viewing and comparing the PDF files 60

Creating a PostScript file 62

Creating a PDF file in two steps 70

Review 72

Electronic Publishing   **Lesson 4**
with Adobe Acrobat
On-screen viewing versus printing on demand 76

Electronic publishing tools 78

Publishing on the World Wide Web 79

Making document design decisions 81

Review 83

Using and Creating Navigational Structures

Lesson 5

Opening the work file 88

Using bookmarks 88

Using thumbnails 97

Creating a cross-document link 102

Replacing a page 103

Using articles 105

Review 109

Modifying PDF Documents

Lesson 6

Opening and examining the work file 114

Automatically generating links and bookmarks 115

Editing pages 116

Editing text 126

Using links and bookmarks to play actions 129

Review 133

Creating an Online Version of a Book

Project

About this project 138

Setting Distiller options 138

Creating the PDF file 141

Viewing the distilled PDF file 142

Adding bookmarks 144

Creating an article thread 149

Replacing a page 154

Comparing different online versions of the same book ..155

Review 157

Adding Page Actions, Movies, and Sound to PDF Files

Lesson 7

Using movie and sound files 162

Opening the work file 162

Using page actions 163

Using movies in PDF files 164

Using sounds in a document 170

Review 173

Adding Buttons

Lesson 8

Using and adding buttons 178

Using the Show-Hide Field action 187

Adding a text-only button that links to
the World Wide Web 190

Determining the opening display of a document 192

Review 193

Creating Forms

Lesson 9

Working with forms online 198

Adding form fields 201

Creating a Submit Form data field 210

Creating a Reset Form field 211

Filling out the fields 212

Review 212

Multimedia Project

Project

About this multimedia project 218

Opening the work file 218

Adding a Go to View button 219

Adding more buttons and page actions 222

Choosing the opening view 228

Review 232

Using Exchange in a Document Review Cycle

Lesson 10

Opening the work file 236

Using notes 236

Capturing a fax image file (Windows only) 240

Correcting suspects (Windows only) 242

Setting file security 243

Review 245

Building a Searchable PDF Library

Lesson 11

Building an index 250

Searching an index 254

Using Document Info fields to search 260

Searching with Boolean expressions 262

Searching on the Web 263

Review 263

Distributing PDF Documents

Project

Distributing PDF documents 268

Comparing compression option results 273

Examining sample *Welcome* documents 276

Adding Document Info data to PDF files 279

Organizing your staging area 280

Optimizing PDF documents 280

Indexing your document collection 282

Including Acrobat Reader installers 285

Double-checking the checklist 285

Review 286

Review Questions & Answers 289

Index 301

Introduction

Adobe Acrobat software is a collection of programs that let you create and modify electronic documents in Portable Document Format, or PDF. Acrobat gives you the ability to create a PDF document from either an electronic or paper file, while maintaining the appearance and design integrity of the original document. A variety of tools and features let you add interactive elements to your document, from custom hyperlinks and media clips to form fields and buttons. You can also use Acrobat to create a searchable electronic library of files and place security locks on files to be circulated.

Prerequisites

Before beginning to use *Adobe Acrobat Classroom in a Book®*, you should have a working knowledge of your operating system and its conventions. In particular, you should know how to do the following:

- Use a mouse and standard Windows® or Macintosh® menus and commands.
- Open, save, and close files.
- Resize and position application and document windows on the screen.

For help with any of these techniques, please see your Windows or Macintosh documentation.

About Classroom in a Book

Adobe Acrobat Classroom in a Book is designed for beginning users of Adobe Acrobat. In this book, you'll learn the fundamental concepts and features you'll need to know to make the most of the Acrobat suite of programs.

Adobe Acrobat Classroom in a Book is divided into a number of self-contained lessons, each covering the basic concepts and techniques associated with a group of Acrobat features. In addition to the lessons, *Adobe Acrobat Classroom in a Book* contains several projects that guide you through the process of assembling larger electronic publications and give you a chance to practice the skills you've learned in previous lessons. If you've never used Acrobat before, you should first complete Lesson 1, "Introduction to Adobe Acrobat Exchange 3.0," before beginning any of the other lessons or projects.

Each lesson and project concludes with review questions summarizing what you've covered. Taking time to answer the review questions will help you retain important concepts about the lesson and about Acrobat. Answers to all the review questions can be found at the end of this book.

System requirements

Classroom in a Book can be used on a PC that runs Windows or on a Macintosh. In addition to the system requirements for either system, you need Adobe Acrobat 3.0 and a CD-ROM drive to use the Classroom in a Book files. To complete *Acrobat Classroom in a Book,* you need the following hardware or software, according to your system and platform:

Windows 95:

- 486, or Pentium® processor-based personal computer
- Microsoft® Windows 95
- 8 MB of RAM for Acrobat Exchange
- 8 MB of RAM for Acrobat® Catalog
- 16 MB of RAM for Acrobat® Distiller
- 16 MB of RAM for Acrobat Capture® plug-in (requires 486 or Pentium processor-based personal computer)
- CD-ROM drive

Windows® NT 3.5.1 and later:

- 386, 486, or Pentium processor-based personal computer
- Windows NT 3.5.1, Windows NT 4.0, or later
- 16 MB of RAM for Acrobat Exchange
- 16 MB of RAM for Acrobat Catalog
- 24 MB of RAM for Acrobat Distiller
- 24 MB of RAM for Acrobat Capture plug-in (requires 486 or Pentium processor-based personal computer)
- CD-ROM drive

Macintosh 68020 – 68040:

- 4 MB of RAM available to Acrobat Exchange
- 6 MB of RAM available to Acrobat Catalog
- 6 MB of RAM available to Acrobat Distiller
- Apple® system software 7.0 or later
- CD-ROM drive

Power Macintosh®:

- 6 MB of RAM available to Acrobat Exchange
- 8 MB of RAM available to Acrobat Catalog
- 8 MB of RAM available to Acrobat Distiller
- Apple system software 7.0 or later
- CD-ROM drive

Note: *At the time of publication, the Import, Scan, and Capture plug-ins were available only for the Windows 95 and Windows NT 3.5.1 versions of Acrobat 3.0.*

Playing movies and sounds

If you're using Acrobat on a Windows or Macintosh system, you can play movies and sounds that have been added to a PDF document. To play movies or sounds, you need the following hardware and software:

- In Windows, you need to have the appropriate sound and video boards installed on your system and Apple QuickTime® 2.0 (or later) software.
- On the Macintosh, you need Apple QuickTime 2.0 or later.

QuickTime software is included as an installation option in the Acrobat 3.0 installer.

Adobe Acrobat Classroom in a Book package contents

The *Adobe Acrobat Classroom in a Book* package includes the following software and documentation:

- *Adobe Acrobat Classroom in a Book*

• The Adobe Acrobat Classroom in a Book CD-ROM containing the lesson practice files, tour movies of other Adobe products, and the *Electronic Publishing Guide,* which provides a comprehensive guide to publishing electronic documents with Acrobat.

To explore the Acrobat Classroom in a Book CD-ROM:

1 Insert the Acrobat Classroom in a Book CD-ROM into your CD-ROM drive.

2 Open the Contents.pdf file, located on the CD-ROM.

The Contents.pdf file contains an interactive shell that lets you explore the various documents and movies included on the CD-ROM. Click the desired document or movie name to view it.

Getting started

If you haven't already done so, install Adobe Acrobat 3.0. For more information, see the *Getting Started* documentation included in the Acrobat software package.

If you've never used Acrobat before, it may be helpful to watch the tour movie located on the Acrobat program CD-ROM. You may also want to do the step-by-step Acrobat tutorials, also located on the program CD-ROM.

Copy the Classroom in a Book files

The Classroom in a Book CD-ROM includes folders containing all the electronic practice files for the Classroom in a Book lessons. Each lesson has its own folder. You must install these folders on your hard disk to use the files for the lessons. To save room on your hard disk, you can install the folders for each lesson as you need them.

To install the Classroom in a Book files for Windows:

1 Create a folder on your hard disk and name it AA3_CIB.

2 Insert the Adobe Acrobat Classroom in a Book CD-ROM into your CD-ROM drive.

3 Open the Lessons folder, located on the CD-ROM.

You should see a folder for each lesson.

4 Copy the desired lesson folder or folders into the AA3_CIB folder.

To install the Classroom in a Book files for the Macintosh:

1 Create a folder on your hard disk and name it Adobe Acrobat CIB.

2 Insert the Adobe Acrobat Classroom in a Book CD-ROM into your CD-ROM drive.

3 Open the Lessons folder, located on the CD-ROM.

You should see a folder for each lesson.

4 Drag the desired lesson folder or folders into the Adobe Acrobat CIB folder.

Create a PROJECTS folder

Throughout the lessons, you'll be prompted to save your practice file in the PROJECTS folder. To do this, you first need to create a subdirectory or folder on your hard disk and name it PROJECTS. It's important that you save your practice files in this folder when prompted, since you'll be using the files in the PROJECTS folder to complete the project, "Distributing PDF Documents."

In a few cases, you will be asked to save your practice file to a location other than the PROJECTS folder, in order to preserve special links in the file. It's important that you always save your practice file in the exact location indicated by the instructions.

Install the Classroom in a Book fonts

To ensure that the lesson files appear on your system with the correct fonts, you need to install the Classroom in a Book font files using the version of Adobe Type Manager® (ATM) that was included in the Acrobat 3.0 software package. These fonts are located in the Fonts folder on the Acrobat Classroom in a Book CD-ROM. For instructions on installing ATM and adding Type 1 fonts to your system, see *Adobe Acrobat 3.0 Getting Started.*

Note: *If you are using Windows NT, install the Classroom in a Book fonts using ATM 4.0. ATM 4.0 is sold separately from the Acrobat 3.0 software package.*

Other resources

Classroom in a Book is not meant to replace the documentation that comes with Adobe Acrobat. Only the commands and features used in the lessons are explained in this book.

For comprehensive information about all of Acrobat's features, refer to the online user guides included with the program. To open an online guide while running Acrobat, choose the desired guide from the Help menu (Windows) or the Balloon Help menu (Macintosh). This menu lists online guides for each component of Adobe Acrobat, as well as the general *Acrobat Online Guide*, which contains a table of contents that leads you to the appropriate component guide.

About Adobe products and services

For more information about Adobe products and services, you can use forums on CompuServe® and America Online℠, the Adobe Home Page on the World Wide Web, or Adobe's own bulletin board system.

To use the Adobe bulletin board, call 206-623-6984. Forums and availability vary by country.

To open the Adobe Home Page from the World Wide Web, use the URL http://www.adobe.com. To launch specific web pages from within Acrobat containing information relevant to Acrobat, choose the desired link from the Help menu (Windows) or from the Balloon Help menu (Macintosh).

Training for the Adobe Certified Expert ™ (ACE) program is available through Adobe Authorized Learning Providers (AALP) and self-study. The ACE program is designed to validate an expert skill level of Adobe products. Careful testing of candidates ensures that each ACE has demonstrated expert product knowledge of the current release of Adobe products, resulting in increased marketability and an added credential.For more information about this program, send e-mail to certification@adobe.com or visit the Adobe Web site at http://www.adobe.com.

1

Lesson 1

Introduction to Adobe Acrobat Exchange 3.0

This interactive tour of Adobe Acrobat provides an overview of the key features of Acrobat Exchange 3.0. You will learn about the basic techniques used to browse a PDF document and about the basic interactive elements that you can add to your documents to make them effective and easy to use. The lessons following this one go over these features, and others, in more detail.

In this lesson, you will learn how to do the following:

• Navigate a document using the buttons in the Acrobat Exchange 3.0 toolbar.

• Change the magnification of a page view.

• Follow a link.

• Display and use bookmarks and thumbnails.

• Activate a movie clip.

• View a note.

• Search for a specified word in a document.

• Fill out an electronic form.

This lesson will take about 35 minutes to complete.

About Adobe Acrobat

Adobe Acrobat is a collection of software programs that lets you view, create, modify, and enhance PDF documents. Based on the PostScript® programming language, PDF (Portable Document Format) is a flexible, cross-platform file format that accurately displays and preserves fonts, page layouts, and other graphical elements in a document.

The Adobe Acrobat product suite includes the following:

• Acrobat Reader lets you view PDF documents. You can download this viewer for free on all platforms from the Adobe Systems Home Page at http://www.adobe.com/prodindex/acrobat/readstep.html.

• Acrobat Exchange lets you modify, as well as view, PDF documents, giving them state-of-the-art electronic document features such as password protection, hypertext links, electronic bookmarks, media clips, and interactive forms. You'll be using Exchange in most of the lessons in this book.

• PDF Writer lets you convert simple documents, such as those created with word-processing or spreadsheet programs, to PDF documents. For information on using PDF Writer, see Lesson 3.

• Acrobat Distiller lets you convert more complex documents, such as those created with drawing, page layout, or image-editing programs, to PDF documents. Lesson 3 provides step-by-step instructions for creating PDF documents with Distiller.

• The Acrobat Capture, Scan, and Import plug-ins to Exchange let you convert scanned paper documents into portable, searchable PDF pages. Lesson 10 covers these features in detail.

Note: *At the time of publication, the Capture, Scan, and Import plug-ins were available only for the Windows 95 and Windows NT 3.5.1 versions of Acrobat 3.0.*

• Acrobat Catalog lets you create a full-text index of a collection of PDF documents. You can then use this index to search the document collection using the search query tool in Exchange or Reader. You'll use Catalog to build a searchable PDF library in Lesson 11.

Publishing PDF documents

Publishing a PDF document involves several steps. First, convert your source documents to PDF—these sources may be electronic files designed in a layout or graphics application, or paper documents that have been scanned into a computer. Once you've compiled your pages in PDF, you can add interactive features such as links, buttons, and multimedia content. If you have a large collection of PDF documents, you may want to use Acrobat Catalog to index the files for quick searching. Finally, prepare the resources and media you need to distribute your PDF publication electronically.

The following illustration summarizes the work-flow process for publishing a PDF document, along with the Acrobat tools used for each step in the process.

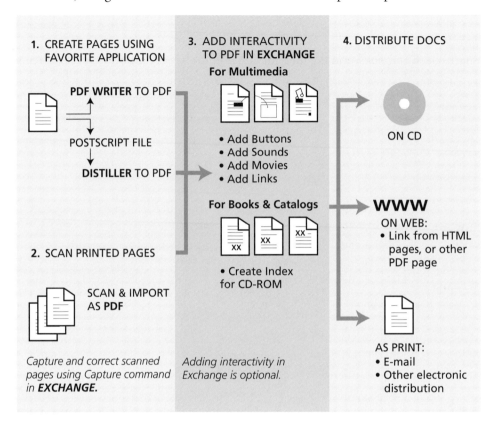

Opening the work file

You'll look at some of Acrobat's basic features as they appear in a fictitious online catalog for outdoor recreational equipment. This publication was designed using illustration and page layout software, and then converted to PDF using Acrobat Distiller.

1 Start Acrobat Exchange.

2 Choose File > Open, select the Utahgear.pdf file, located in the Lesson01 folder, and click Open.

Looking at the work area

The Acrobat Exchange work area consists of the command menus at the top of the screen, the toolbar containing various tools and button controls, the document window containing the active document, the overview window containing bookmarks or thumbnails, and the informational status bar at the bottom of the screen.

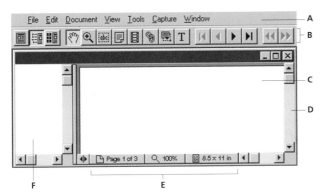

A. Menu bar B. Toolbar C. Document window D. Scroll bar
E. Status bar F. Overview window

Navigating the document

You can navigate through a PDF document using a variety of methods. In addition to turning pages as in a traditional book, you can enlarge the magnification of the page you are viewing and return easily to previous page views.

Looking at the status bar

The status bar at the bottom of the document window tells you about the number of pages in the document, the magnification of the page view displayed on your monitor, and the actual print size of the pages.

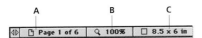

A. Page number B. Magnification C. Page dimensions

Notice that the Utah Gear brochure contains a total of six pages and that you are viewing the first page at 100% magnification. The printed page size of the brochure is 8.5 by 6 inches.

Using the browse buttons

The browse buttons in the toolbar at the top of the window let you page through a document intuitively.

1 Click the Next Page button (▶).

The second page of the catalog appears, as indicated in the page-number box in the status bar.

2 Click the Next Page button several more times to advance to the end of the catalog.

3 Click the Previous Page button (◀) to turn to the preceding page. Click Previous Page several more times to page backwards through the catalog.

Acrobat also has buttons for jumping to the first and last pages of a document.

4 Click the Last Page button (▶|). You are now at the end of the catalog.

5 Click the First Page button (|◀) to return to the start of the document.

Changing the view magnification

The Utah Gear brochure is currently set at 100% view. You can change the magnification of the page view using built-in controls in the toolbar, or by clicking or dragging in the page with the zoom tool.

1 Click the Fit Page button (▣) in the toolbar.

This control fits the entire document page in the document window. Notice that the new magnification appears in the status bar.

2 Click the Next Page button to move to the next page. Notice that the magnification stays the same. This magnification is an example of a *sticky-state* action—its original setting remains even as you change pages.

Next you'll use the zoom tool to magnify a specific portion of a page.

3 Click the zoom tool (🔍) in the toolbar to select it.

4 Drag a rectangle around the text block on page 2 to magnify that area. This is called *marquee-zooming*.

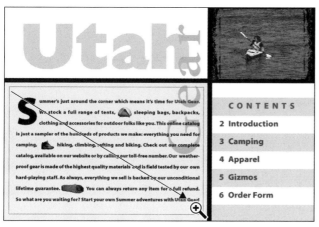

Marquee-zooming

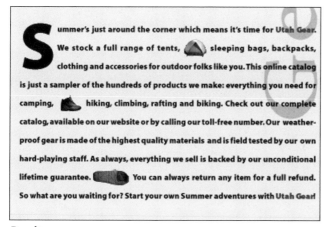

Result

Zooming allows you to increase or decrease the magnification of the page to give you a comfortable page view for reading the document on-screen.

5 Hold down Ctrl (Windows) or Option (Macintosh) to activate the zoom-out pointer (the plus sign inside the magnifying glass turns into a minus sign). Then click once to zoom out.

6 Release Ctrl or Option to return to the zoom-in pointer; then click the first line in the text block to magnify the page again.

Notice that the magnified area centers around the point you clicked. Clicking with the zoom tool is another way to magnify your page view. In Lesson 2, you'll learn how to magnify a page using the magnification box in the status bar.

Following a link

The Utah Gear brochure contains a number of links to other pages in the document that make it easy for you to locate information and navigate through the document. You use the hand tool to follow links.

You should be viewing the magnified text area on page 2 of the brochure.

1 Click the hand tool (🖐) and move the pointer over the picture of the tent. The pointer changes to a pointing finger icon (👆), indicating that you are positioned over a link.

2 Click the picture of the tent to jump to the link destination—a magnified view of page 3, the tent catalog page.

Retracing your viewing path

In Acrobat, a *view* consists of a specific page and a specific magnification displayed on your screen. Acrobat's links and interactive features let you jump quickly and easily to different views. To get back to a previous page view, you use the Go Back button in the toolbar.

The Go Back button is useful for retracing your viewing path through a document, especially when you have followed a complex series of links and changed magnification levels several times.

1 Click the Go Back (◀◀) button. Notice that you have returned to page 2, the page you were viewing before you clicked the tent link.

2 Click Go Back again to return to the page magnification you were viewing before you clicked with the zoom tool.

You can click the Go Back button repeatedly to retrace your viewing path, view by view for up to 64 views, through a document. If you have followed a link to another PDF document, the Go Back button can also return you to your original document.

3 Now click the Go Forward (▶▶) button to reverse the action of your last Go Back. Continue clicking Go Forward until this button dims. You should be viewing the magnified view of page 3 once again.

You use the Go Forward button to return, view by view, to the page where you first used Go Back.

Using bookmarks and thumbnails

Bookmarks and thumbnails help you navigate, organize, and edit PDF documents. These features appear in an overview window to the left of the document window.

1 Click the Bookmarks and Page button (⊞) in the toolbar.

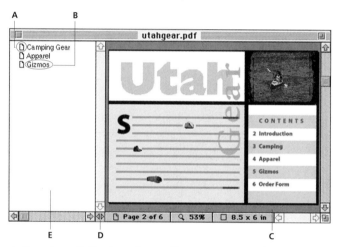

A. Page icon **B.** *Bookmark text* **C.** *Document window* **D.** *Resize box* **E.** *Overview window*

Bookmarks for different topics in the document appear in the overview window to the left of the document window. These bookmarks were created manually to organize and link to the main topics in the document. Bookmarks serve well as a table of contents, and can be rearranged, nested, or renamed to reflect the organization of the document.

If needed, you can scroll through the bookmarks using the scroll bar in the overview window, and you can resize the window by dragging the resize box at the lower right corner of the overview window.

2 Click the Apparel bookmark text to jump to page 4 of the brochure. (Be sure to click the text, and not the icon to its left.)

As you can see, bookmarks and links work similarly.

3 Now click the Thumbnails and Page button (⬛) to display thumbnails for each document page in the overview window.

4 If needed, use the scroll bar for the overview window to bring the thumbnail for page 5 into view. Then click the page 5 thumbnail. (Be sure to click the thumbnail image, not the page-number box below the thumbnail.)

Page 5 appears in the document window, and the page-number box for this thumb-nail becomes highlighted.

5 Now click the thumbnail for page 2 to go to that page (if needed, scroll through the overview window to bring the thumbnail into view). Then click the Page Only button (⬛) in the toolbar to close the overview window.

Watching a movie

Using Acrobat Exchange, you can attach dynamic movie and sound clips to a PDF document. You assign media clips to be activated by links or bookmarks, or whenever the user turns to a specific page in the document.

You should be viewing page 2 of the brochure, and the hand tool should be selected in the toolbar.

1 Click the Actual Page button (▣) to view the page at 100% magnification.

2 Move the pointer over the picture of the kayaker in the upper right corner of the page.

Notice that the pointer changes to a filmstrip icon (▤), indicating that a sound or movie clip can be activated.

3 Click to play the movie. If you want to stop the movie before it finishes, click again in the movie or press the Esc key.

You can attach and play movies and sounds in a PDF document. However, you cannot edit the content of these media clips from within Exchange. For more information about using media clips in a PDF document, see Lesson 7.

Looking at a note

Notes let you add comments to a PDF document to communicate review notes or last-minute information to others, or personal information to yourself. Notes from two reviewers have already been collated in the Utah Gear brochure.

1 Choose Tools > Find Next Note to jump to the first note in the brochure.

Page 3, which contains two notes, appears in the document window.

2 Double-click the highlighted red note to open it.

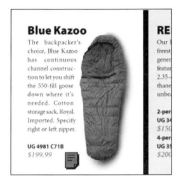

Note closed   *Note opened*

3 After you have read the note, click the close box of the note window to close it.

4 Now double-click the green note to read it. Notes can be set to different colors to identify different note authors. Close the green note when you are finished viewing it.

You will learn more about using notes in Lesson 10.

Searching for a word

Acrobat gives you the following ways to search through a file or a collection of files for a desired piece of information:

• The find tool in Exchange and Reader lets you search through a single document for occurrences of a specific word or phrase.

• The search query tool lets you search for information in a collection of documents, using an index that has been created in Acrobat Catalog.

In this part of the lesson, you'll use the find tool to locate information on water-proof items in the Utah Gear catalog.

1 Click the find tool (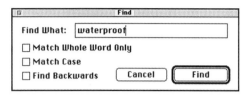) in the toolbar to display the Find dialog box.

The Find dialog box lets you enter the word or phrase you want to find.

2 For Find What, enter **waterproof.**

3 If needed, deselect the Match Whole Word Only option and the Match Case option. Deselecting these options displays all occurrences of "waterproof," regardless of whether it appears within another word, or in uppercase or lowercase characters. The Find Backwards option lets you search backwards starting from the current page in the document.

4 Click Find to begin the search.

The word "waterproofing" appears highlighted on page 3.

The find tool in Exchange suffices when you want to search for a word or phrase in a single document. For more sophisticated searching of multiple documents at once, you can use the Search command. Lesson 11 covers the Search command in detail.

Filling out a form

You can use Acrobat Exchange to create interactive forms for other Acrobat users to fill in. For example, you can create an order form for potential customers or an evaluation form for reviewers of your document. Users can simply print the forms or they can submit them over the World Wide Web. Submitted form data is imported and exported independently of the forms themselves, making for efficient transmission and archiving.

In this part of a lesson, you'll look at an existing electronic form and fill out the form fields with your own information.

1 Click the Last Page button (▶I) to display the order form on page 6. If needed, click the Actual Page button (◻) to set the view at 100%.

Notice that the form fields have been created for you. They include text fields for entering a name and address, and pop-up menus for selecting products.

2 Click the hand tool, and move the pointer inside the field box to the right of Name. Notice that the pointer changes to the I-beam pointer.

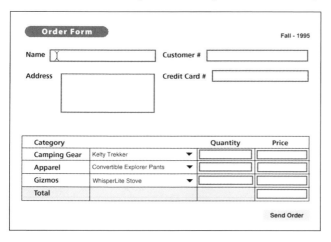

3 Click inside the box to set an insertion point, and type your name.

4 Press the Tab key to advance to the Address field, and type your home address. Press Enter (Windows) or Return (Macintosh) when you want to start a new line.

5 Now position the pointer over the arrow in the Camping Gear line. Click the mouse button (Windows) or hold down the mouse button (Macintosh), and choose Therm-a-Rest from the pop-up menu.

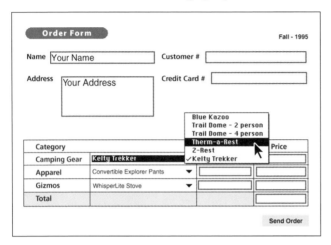

This pop-up menu, or *combo box,* lets you choose one item from a prearranged list.

6 Continue to choose items from the Apparel and Gizmos combo boxes.

7 Choose File > Save As, name your file 01work.pdf, and save it in your PROJECTS folder.

8 Choose File > Close to close the document.

Lesson 9 covers creating form fields in detail.

Review

This lesson introduced you to the basic navigational techniques and interactive elements that you can use and add to a PDF document. The following lessons and projects provide in-depth instructions for creating the elements mentioned here, as well as for using and creating other elements still to be introduced. For a brief description of the features covered in each lesson, scan the lesson titles in the Table of Contents.

To test your knowledge of the concepts and techniques you learned in this lesson, answer the following questions:

- How do you return to a previous view of a PDF document?

- What kind of document information is displayed in the status bar?

- How do you navigate to a page using thumbnails?

- What is the difference between the find tool and the Search command?

- What features are displayed in the overview window?

- What key do you press to activate the zoom-out tool?

- How do you activate a movie clip?

- How do you access the Acrobat online guides? (For the answer, see the Introduction.)

2

Lesson 2

Navigating and Linking

In this lesson, you'll learn how to navigate through a PDF document. You'll page through an online magazine using controls built into Adobe Acrobat, and create your own custom navigational controls to link from one section of the magazine to another.

In this lesson, you'll learn how to do the following:

- Page through a PDF document using Acrobat's built-in navigational controls.
- Change the page layout of a document as it appears on-screen.
- Change the magnification of a view.
- Create and edit links to different views within a document.
- Retrace your viewing path through a document.
- Create a link to a site on the World Wide Web.

This lesson will take about 40 minutes to complete.

About navigation

Acrobat Exchange and Reader contain built-in navigational controls in the menu, tool, status, and scroll bars that let you browse a PDF document page by page, or quickly jump to a specific page of the document. Using these controls, you can view a PDF document much as you would view a printed book, while taking advantage of the greater speed and efficiency of electronic navigation.

In addition to these built-in controls, Acrobat Exchange lets you create custom navigational controls in your document. These controls include links, bookmarks, thumbnails, and article threads. Bookmarks, thumbnails, and articles are discussed in Lesson 5, while other controls such as buttons and page actions are discussed in Lessons 7 and 8.

Opening the work file

You'll practice navigating through a fictional online magazine called *Digital Arts*. *Digital Arts* is a glossy, tabloid-style magazine that contains the hottest news in the computer world. In addition to buying the printed magazine from newsstands, readers can view and download the electronic version.

Digital Arts was created using Adobe PageMaker®, and then converted to PDF.

1 Start Acrobat Exchange.

2 Choose File > Open.

3 Select Digarts.pdf, located in the Lesson02 folder, and click Open.

About on-screen display

Take a look at the status bar, located at the bottom of the document window. Notice that the magazine is tabloid size (11 inches x 17 inches) and currently appears at 100% magnification on-screen.

The magnification shown in the status bar does not refer to the printed size of the page, but rather to how the page is displayed on-screen. Acrobat determines the on-screen display of a page by treating the page as a 72 ppi (pixels-per-inch) image. For example, if your page has a print size of 2 inches by 2 inches, Acrobat treats the page as if it were 144 pixels wide and 144 pixels high (72 x 2 = 144). At 100% view, each pixel in the page is represented by one screen pixel on your monitor.

How large the page actually appears on-screen depends on your monitor size and your monitor resolution setting. For example, when you increase the resolution of your monitor, you increase the number of screen pixels within the same monitor area; this results in smaller screen pixels and a smaller displayed page, since the number of pixels in the page itself stays constant. The following illustration shows the variation among 100% displays of the same page on different monitors.

PIXEL DIMENSIONS AND MONITOR RESOLUTION Regardless of the print size specified for an image, the size of an image on-screen is determined by the pixel dimensions of the image and the monitor size and setting. A large monitor set to 640 by 480 pixels uses larger pixels than a small monitor with the same setting. In most cases, default Macintosh monitor settings are designed to display approximately 72 pixels per inch; default PC monitor settings typically display 96 pixels per inch.

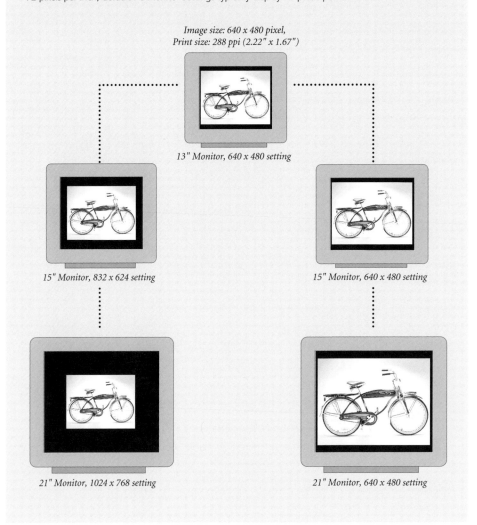

Image size: 640 x 480 pixel,
Print size: 288 ppi (2.22" x 1.67")

13" Monitor, 640 x 480 setting

15" Monitor, 832 x 624 setting

15" Monitor, 640 x 480 setting

21" Monitor, 1024 x 768 setting

21" Monitor, 640 x 480 setting

Navigating the magazine

Exchange provides a variety of ways for you to move through and adjust the magnification of a document. For example, you can scroll through the magazine using the scroll bar at the right side of the window, or you can turn pages as in a traditional book using the browse buttons in the toolbar. You can also jump to a specific page using the status bar at the bottom of the window.

Browsing the document

1 If needed, click the hand tool to select it. Move your pointer over the image at the right of the page and hold down the mouse button.

The open hand changes to a closed hand when you hold down the mouse.

2 Drag the hand in the window to move the page around on the screen. This is similar to moving a piece of paper around on a desktop.

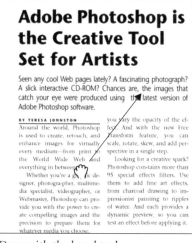

Drag with the hand tool...   *to move the page.*

3 Press Enter (Windows) or Return (Macintosh) to display the next part of the page. You can press Enter or Return repeatedly to view the document from start to finish in screen-sized sections.

4 Click the Fit Page button (▣) in the toolbar to view the entire page on your monitor. If needed, click the First Page button (◀) to view page 1.

5 Position the pointer over the down arrow in the scroll bar, and click once.

The document scrolls automatically to display all of page 2. You can control how PDF pages scroll and display in the document window.

6 Position the pointer over the page-size box in the status bar, and click (Windows) or hold down the mouse (Macintosh) to view the page layout pop-up menu. Notice that the Single Page layout option is currently chosen.

7 Choose Continuous from the pop-up menu. Then use the scroll bar to scroll to page 3.

The Continuous option displays pages end to end like frames in a filmstrip.

8 Now choose Continuous - Facing Pages from the page layout menu to display page spreads, with left- and right-hand pages facing each other, as on a layout board. Press Enter (Windows) or Return (Macintosh) several times to view the different pages.

In keeping with the conventions of printed books, a PDF document always begins with a right-hand page.

9 Reset the layout to Single Page.

You can use the page-number box in the status bar to switch directly to a specific page.

10 Click the page-number box in the status bar to display the Go To Page dialog box.

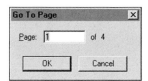

11 Type **4** and click OK.

You are now viewing page 4 of *Digital Arts*. The scroll bar also lets you navigate to a specific page.

12 Begin dragging the scroll box in the scroll bar. As you drag, a page status box appears. When page 1 appears in the status box, release the mouse.

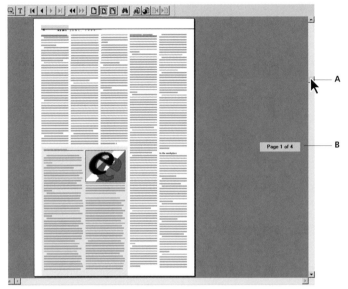

A. *Scroll box* **B.** *Page status box*

You should now be back at the beginning of *Digital Arts*.

Changing the view magnification

You can change the magnification of the page view using controls in the toolbar and status bar, or by clicking or dragging in the page with the zoom tool.

1 Click the Fit Width button (⬛) in the toolbar.

This control adjusts the magnification to spread the page across the whole width of your screen. Notice that a new magnification appears in the status bar.

2 Click the Next Page button (▶) to advance to page 2. Notice that the magnification remains the same.

3 Click the Actual Size button (⬛) to return the page to 100% view.

4 Place the pointer over the magnification box in the status bar, and hold down the mouse button to display the pop-up menu of preset magnifications. Drag to choose 200% for the magnification.

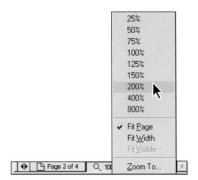

You can also enter a specific value for the magnification.

5 Click the magnification box in the status bar to display the Zoom To dialog box. Enter **75** and click OK.

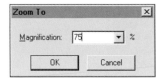

6 Now click the Fit Page button (▢) to display the whole page in the window. Clicking Fit Page gives you an overview of the page contents and layout.

Next you'll use the zoom tool to magnify a specific portion of a page.

7 Click the page-number box in the status bar, enter **3** in the Go To Page dialog box, and click OK. Then click the zoom tool (🔍) in the toolbar.

8 Click in the top right section of the page to double the magnification. Notice that the view centers around the point you clicked. Click in the top right of the page again to double the magnification one more time.

9 Now press Ctrl (Windows) or Option (Macintosh). Notice that the zoom pointer now appears with a minus sign, indicating that the zoom-out tool is active.

10 With Ctrl or Option pressed, click in the document to cut the magnification by one half. Ctrl- or Option-click again to halve the magnification again. Then release Ctrl or Option.

The entire page should fit on your screen again. Now you'll drag the zoom tool to magnify the Contents area.

11 Place the pointer near the top left of the Contents section, and drag over the text as shown in the illustration.

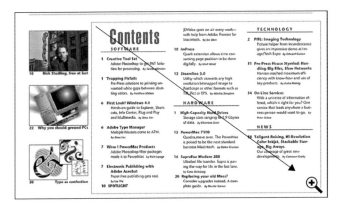

The view zooms in on the area you enclosed. This is called *marquee-zooming*.

Using and creating links

In a PDF document, you don't always have to view pages in sequence. You can jump immediately from one section of a document to another using custom navigational aids such as *links*.

One benefit of placing *Digital Arts* online is that you can convert traditional cross-references into links, which users can use to jump directly to the referenced section or file. For example, you can make each item under the contents list of *Digital Arts* into a link that jumps to its corresponding section. You can also use links to add interactivity to traditional book elements such as tables of contents or indexes.

Following a link

You'll test out an existing link before creating your own. You should be viewing the Contents section at the bottom of page 3.

1 Click the hand tool in the toolbar.

2 Move the pointer over Trapping Pitfalls in the Contents section so that the pointing finger appears, and click to follow the link.

This item links to the trapping section at the bottom of the first page.

3 Click the Go Back button (◀◀) to return to your previous view of the Contents section.

You can click Go Back at any time to retrace your viewing path through a document. The Go Forward button (▶▶) lets you reverse the action of your last Go Back.

Creating a link

Now you'll create a link around the PIFL: Imaging Technology listing in the Contents to the corresponding article in the magazine.

You use the link tool to create new links in a document. To specify an activation area, or *hot spot,* for the link, you drag over the desired area with the link tool. Then you set the destination view for the link.

1 Click the link tool (🖐) in the toolbar.

The link tool appears as a crosshair pointer when you move it into the document. When you select the link tool, all the existing links in the document appear temporarily as black rectangles.

2 Place the cross hair above and to the left of the PIFL: Imaging Technologies listing in the third column of the Contents, and drag down as shown in the illustration to create a marquee that encloses the entire text block.

The Create Link dialog box appears. This dialog box lets you specify the appearance of the hot spot as well as the link action.

3 Under Appearance, for Type, choose Invisible Rectangle.

4 Under Action, for Type, choose Go to View.

The Go to View option lets you specify a page view as the destination for the link. The Go to View action is just one among many actions that you can assign to your link. For complete information on the different action types, see the *Exchange Online Guide.*

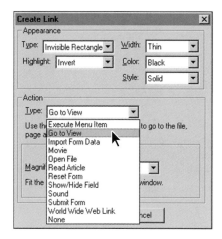

5 With the Create Link dialog box still open, click the Previous Page button (◀) to go to page 2 of *Digital Arts.* The section on PIFL imaging is at the top of this page.

6 In the Create Link dialog box, for Magnification, choose Fit Width.

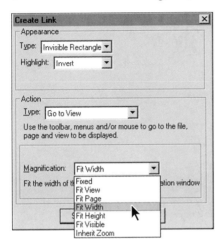

7 Click Set Link. The page view returns to the Contents section.

You have now created a link from the Contents to page 2, whose view will fill the width of the screen when the link is activated.

8 Select the hand tool, and move the pointer over the PIFL: Imaging Technologies listing in the Contents. Notice that the pointing finger indicates the hot spot you've just created.

9 Click the hot spot to test your link. You should jump to the PIFL section with a Fit Width magnification view.

10 Click Go Back to return to the Contents.

11 Choose File > Save As, name the document 02work.pdf, and save it in your PROJECTS folder.

Next, you'll edit an existing link in the Contents.

Editing a link

You can edit a link at any time by changing its appearance, hot spot area, or link action.

1 Click the hand tool in the toolbar, and click the Creative Tool Set listing to follow its link.

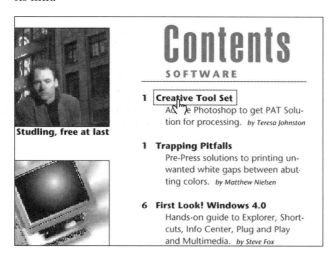

Notice that the link does not link to the correct section. You'll edit the destination of this link and make the link appearance invisible.

2 Click Go Back to return to the Contents.

3 Click the link tool, and then double-click inside the black rectangle surrounding Creative Tool Set to open the Link Properties dialog box.

This dialog box lets you edit the appearance and destination of the selected link.

4 Under Appearance, for Type, choose Invisible Rectangle.

5 Click Edit Destination.

6 Click the First Page button (◄) to navigate to the beginning of *Digital Arts*, where the section entitled "Adobe Photoshop is the Creative Tool Set for Artists" appears.

7 If needed, drag the Link Properties dialog box out of the way, and click the Fit Page button (▢).

8 Click the zoom tool (⊕)and drag a marquee to enlarge the story, as shown in the following illustration.

9 In the Link Properties dialog box, for Magnification, choose Fixed.

The Fixed option sets the link destination at the current magnification displayed on your screen.

10 Click Set Link.

11 Click the hand tool, and click the Creative Tool Set listing to test your revised link.

You should jump to the enlarged view of the correct story on page 1.

12 Click the Go Back button (◀◀) to return to the Contents.

Now you'll expand the linked area around Creative Tool Set so that it encompasses the entire text block.

13 Click the link tool (✎) in the toolbar, and click inside the rectangle surrounding Creative Tool Set.

Handles appear at the corners of the rectangle, indicating that the link is selected.

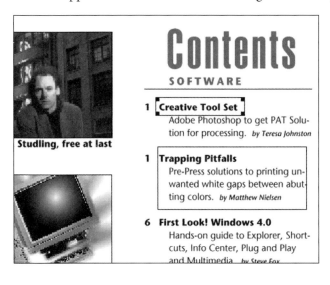

14 Move the pointer over the bottom right handle so that the double-headed arrow appears. Then drag down to stretch the rectangle around the text block under the title.

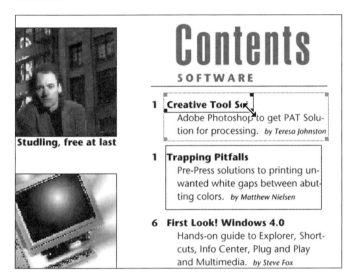

15 Click the hand tool, and move the pointer over the Creative Tool Set listing.

Notice that the hot area includes the entire text block under the listing.

16 Click the hot area to test your link.

Creating a link to a Web site

Earlier you created a link from one area of *Digital Arts* to another. Now you'll add a link that leads to a page on the World Wide Web.

1 Click the Fit Page button (▣) in the toolbar.

2 Click the Next Page button (▶) to advance to page 2.

3 Click the zoom tool (◓) in the toolbar, and click in the cream-colored area at the bottom of the page to enlarge it.

This area of the page contains an advertisement for Adobe Press's Classroom in a Book series. You'll create a link from an image in the ad to Adobe System's Web page, which describes the book series in greater detail.

4 Click the link tool (🖐) in the toolbar, and drag a marquee around the center image of the Adobe Acrobat Classroom in a Book.

The Create Link dialog box appears.

5 Under Appearance, for Type, choose Visible Rectangle.

6 For Width, choose Medium; for Color, choose Red; and for Style, choose Solid.

Now you'll assign the action to link to the World Wide Web. First you'll copy the target URL from the advertisement.

7 Click the select-text tool (⌷abc⌷) in the toolbar.

8 Drag to highlight the URL at the bottom of the ad. Then press Ctrl+C (Windows) or Command+C (Macintosh) to copy the text to the Clipboard.

9 In the Create Link dialog box, for Action Type, choose World Wide Web Link, and click Edit URL.

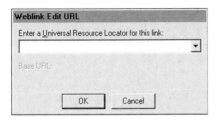

10 Press Ctrl+V (Windows) or Command+V (Macintosh) to paste the URL you just copied, and click OK.

11 Click Set Link.

If you have a Web browser and a connection to the World Wide Web, you can go on to the next step and test your newly created link. First you'll specify a Web browser to use when opening Weblinks. Once you establish your browser preference, Exchange automatically uses that browser to open all Weblinks.

12 Choose File > Preferences > Weblink. Then click Browse (Windows) or Select (Macintosh).

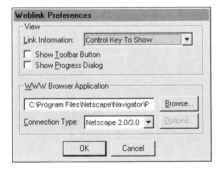

13 Select your browser application, and click Open. Then click OK to return to the document.

14 Use the hand tool to test your Weblink.

This link opens the Adobe Systems Web site using the browser you've just specified. The site opens to the page describing the *Classroom in a Book* series.

15 Close the browser window when you are finished viewing the Web site, and return to Acrobat Exchange.

16 Choose File > Save As, and save 02work.pdf in your PROJECTS folder. Replace the existing 02work.pdf file.

17 Choose File > Close to close the document.

Review

In this lesson, you learned how to page through a PDF document, change the magnification and page layout mode, and create and edit links. In later lessons, you'll learn how to create and use other navigational features such as bookmarks, thumbnails, and article threads.

To test your knowledge of the concepts and techniques you learned in this lesson, answer the following questions:

• Name three ways in which you can switch to a different page.

• Name three ways in which you can change the view magnification.

• What kinds of destinations can a link jump to?

- How do you control the view magnification of a link destination?
- How do you edit an existing link?

3

Lesson 3

Creating PDF Documents

Create PDF documents quickly and easily from your existing electronic files using Acrobat Distiller or PDF Writer 3.0. Your document type, content, and layout determine which component you use to create a PDF file.

In this lesson you will learn how to do the following:

• Use PDF Writer to create a PDF document.

• Use Distiller to create a PDF document.

• Compare the output between PDF documents created with Distiller and PDF Writer.

• Set up a PostScript printer driver.

• Create a PDF file from PageMaker 6.5.

This lesson will take about 40 minutes to complete.

Creating PDF documents

The content of a PDF file must be created in a program other than Acrobat. You can use any of your favorite word-processing, page-layout, graphic, or business programs to create content and then convert those documents to PDF at the time you would normally print to paper. You can think of PDF files as the electronic paper version of your original documents.

Creating PDF files is as easy as printing from your application. You have two "printing" choices, PDF Writer or Distiller. Both are installed as part of the default Acrobat 3.0 installation process. But when should you use one and when the other?

PDF Writer or Distiller?

Your work-flow process, document type, and document content determine which Acrobat producer—PDF Writer or Distiller—you should use to create your PDF document.

Use PDF Writer for quick conversion of simple business documents to PDF. If you do not obtain satisfactory results with PDF Writer, convert the document to PDF with Distiller.

Use Distiller for documents containing Encapsulated PostScript (EPS) graphics, documents containing bitmap images for which you need to choose specific resampling and compression methods, or documents produced from desktop publishing applications, such as Adobe® FrameMaker®, Adobe PageMaker, and QuarkXPress®, that have been optimized to print to PostScript. Also use Distiller for batch processing on your hard drive or over a network.

The following table provides general guidelines to help you determine which producer to select for specific types of documents.

Use Distiller if you:	Use PDF Writer if you:
Have desktop publishing documents such as those created with PageMaker, FrameMaker, QuarkXPress, Illustrator, or Freehand®	Have simple business documents such as those created with Microsoft® Word™ or Excel™
Have documents containing EPS graphics	Have documents that do not contain EPS graphics
Have documents containing images where you need precise control over compression and downsampling options	Embed TrueType™ fonts on Windows 95 or Windows NT and would like to maintain searchable text
Have documents containing PostScript features that you need to maintain in the PDF document such as OPI comments	Want to add a Create PDF macro to applications that use macros
Send documents to Prepress or Service bureaus for high-end publishing	Do not want to install a PostScript printer driver on your system (PostScript printer drivers are required to use Distiller)
Have documents you would like to batch process	Have limited amounts of RAM
Would like to share Distiller on a network server	Want to produce PDF documents quicker than you can with Distiller
Obtain unsatisfactory results from PDF Writer	

Creating a PDF file with PDF Writer

PDF Writer is best used with simple business documents that contain mostly text. The process of using PDF Writer to create a PDF file is usually faster than using Distiller. But in some documents, especially those containing placed EPS images, you may not obtain satisfactory results using PDF Writer. In those cases, use Distiller to process the files.

In this section, you will create a PDF file of a simple document, created in a word processor, using PDF Writer. We have supplied a Microsoft Word document. If your word processor cannot open a Microsoft Word document, skip to the "Viewing the PDF file" on page 58, and use the supplied PDF document.

Opening the work file

1 Start your word processor.

2 Choose File > Open. Locate and select Contract.doc from the list of files in the Lesson03 folder, and click Open. If you receive a message indicating that the necessary fonts are not installed, see "Install the Classroom in a Book Fonts" on page 5, and install the fonts from the Classroom in a Book CD-ROM.

Note: If viewing the document in Word for Windows, the Encapsulated PostScript Import Graphic Filter must be installed to preview the car logo at the top of the page correctly. See your Word for Windows user manual for installation instructions.

Using PDF Writer

Creating a PDF file is as easy as selecting PDF Writer and printing. This section has been organized by platform. Find your platform, follow the steps in that section, then continue with the "Viewing the PDF file" section on page 58.

In Windows:

1 Choose File > Print.

2 Follow the instructions for your Windows platform:

• In Windows NT 3.5.1, select Acrobat PDF Writer on DISK from the Specific Printer menu, and click Print.

Note: At the time of publication, PDF Writer was not available for Windows NT 4.0.

• In Windows 95, select Acrobat PDF Writer 3.0 from the Printer name menu, and click OK.

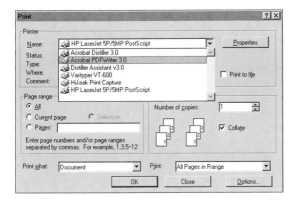

3 Name the PDF document Contract.pdf, save it to the PROJECTS folder, and click OK. The Document Info dialog box appears. Document Info fields are used by search engines to help you categorize documents and provide a descriptive title for search results lists. Searching and search results lists are explained and used in Lesson 11.

4 Enter the following information for Document Info:

• For Title, enter **Sales Agency Agreement**.

• For Subject, enter **Sales**.

• For Author, enter **Legal department**.

• For Keywords, enter **sales, payment, agreement**.

5 Click OK.

6 Exit your word processor.

On the Macintosh:

1 Hold down the shortcut key (the Control key by default) and choose File > Print. The shortcut allows you to access PDF Writer even if a different item is selected in the Chooser.

See "Using the PDF Writer Shortcut" in the *PDF Writer Online Guide* for more information.

2 Select All as the page range, deselect View PDF File, and select Prompt for Document Info, then click OK.

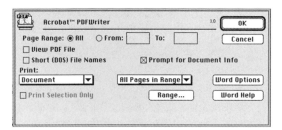

The Document Info dialog box appears. Document Info fields are used by search engines to help you categorize documents and provide a descriptive title for search results lists. Searching and search results lists are explained and used in Lesson 11.

3 Enter the following information for Document Info:

• For Title, enter **Sales Agency Agreement**.

• For Subject, enter **Sales**.

• For Author, enter **Legal department**.

• For Keywords, enter **sales, payment, agreement**.

4 Click OK.

5 Name the PDF document Contract.pdf, save it to the PROJECTS folder, and click Save.

6 Quit your word processor.

Viewing the PDF file

1 Start Exchange.

2 Choose File > Open. Locate and select Contract.pdf from the list of files in the PROJECTS folder, and click Open.

Note: If you need to use the supplied PDF document, locate and open the Supply folder inside the Lesson03 folder, select Contract.pdf from the list of files, and click Open.

Take a moment to look at the document. Notice that PDF Writer has recreated the original document maintaining the format, fonts, and layout.

3 Minimize or hide Exchange.

Creating PDF with Distiller

Acrobat PDF Writer works directly from an application, but Acrobat Distiller requires a PostScript language file to create a PDF file. You can create a PostScript file from almost any application if you have a PostScript printer driver installed on your system. In this section, you will process a PostScript file that we have provided for you with Distiller. Later in this lesson, we provide you with general instructions for creating a PostScript file from any application, and specific instructions to create a PDF file from Adobe PageMaker 6.5.

Converting a PostScript file to PDF

You will convert a PostScript file that was originally created from a PageMaker document. The illustration below shows the original file.

1 Start Distiller.

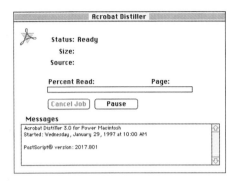

Note: If this is the first time you have launched Distiller since installing Acrobat 3.0, you will be asked to choose between Acrobat 3.0 and Acrobat 2.1 compatibility. Choose Acrobat 3.0 compatibility. For details, see the Distiller Online Guide.

2 Choose File > Open. Locate and select Flyer.ps from the list of files in the Lesson03 folder, and click Open.

3 Enter **Flyer.pdf** as the filename, save it in the PROJECTS folder, and click OK or Save. Distiller converts the file and outputs a PDF file to your PROJECTS folder.

Distiller's default compression and font settings will usually create an acceptably small and efficient PDF file. If you need more control over file size or image quality, you can easily change the default options. See the *Distiller Online Guide* for information about changing the default settings and general guidelines for creating PDF documents with Distiller from all applications.

4 Exit or quit Distiller.

Viewing and comparing the PDF files

Now take a look at the PDF document created by Distiller.

1 Return to Acrobat Exchange.

2 Choose File > Open. Locate and select Flyer.pdf from the list of files in the PROJECTS folder, and click Open.

Note: If you need to use the supplied PDF document, locate and open the Supply folder inside the Lesson03 folder, select Flyer.pdf from the list of files, and click Open.

As you can see, Distiller created an exact duplicate of the original file as shown in the illustration on page 59. Take particular notice of the car logo at the top of the page. This was a placed Encapsulated PostScript (EPS) image in the PageMaker document. You will now compare it with the PDF document you created with PDF Writer that contains the same logo.

3 If you closed Contract.pdf earlier, open it again.

4 Choose Window > Tile Vertically to view Flyer.pdf and Contract.pdf side by side.

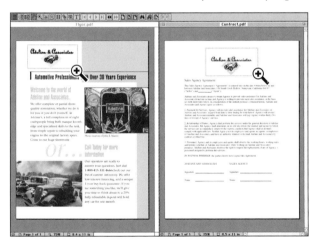

5 Select the zoom tool (🔍) and marquee-zoom around the car logo at the top of the page in each document to magnify the view of the logo.

Notice that the PDF file produced by Acrobat Distiller (Flyer.pdf) displays a cleaner logo than the logo displayed in the Acrobat PDF Writer document (Contract.pdf). Because PDF Writer does not understand the PostScript language, it supplies a bitmap image of placed EPS files in the PDF documents it creates. In contrast,

Acrobat Distiller maintains the resolution independence of the placed EPS graphic because it understands the PostScript information that describes it and passes that along in the PDF file.

Distiller   PDFWriter

6 Now scroll to view the text in each document.

Notice that the text in each document is smooth and easy to read. You can use either Distiller or PDF Writer to get acceptable results from text-based documents.

7 When you have finished viewing the documents, choose Window > Close All to close the documents.

If you are interested in learning how to create a PostScript file from almost any application, and how to create one specifically from PageMaker 6.5, go on to the next section. Otherwise, skip to the "Review" section on page 72 to answer the review questions.

Creating a PostScript file

As mentioned earlier, Acrobat Distiller requires a PostScript language file to create a PDF file. To create a PostScript file, you need a PostScript printer driver.

A PostScript printer driver translates an electronic document into a form that a PostScript device such as a printer or Acrobat Distiller can use to create a printed page or a PDF file.

Use the Adobe PostScript Printer Driver to create PostScript files for converting to PDF with Acrobat Distiller. You can install this driver from the Adobe Acrobat 3.0 CD-ROM. See *Getting Started with Adobe Acrobat 3.0* for installation instructions.

After installing the driver, you will want to follow the instructions in this lesson to add the Acrobat Distiller PostScript Printer Description (PPD) file. You only have to add the Acrobat Distiller PPD once.

A PPD tells the printer driver what type of device you are printing to and what are the capabilities of that device. In the case of Distiller, the PPD tells the driver to include information such as color and custom page size. If you create a file with color and a custom page size, but chose a PPD that does not let the driver know about those document properties, Distiller will output a black-and-white, 8 1/2-by-11 inch PDF file. So, it is always best to use the PPD for the device to which you are outputting the document.

After setting up the Acrobat Distiller PPD, you can create a PostScript file for converting to PDF with Acrobat Distiller.

This section of the lesson is separated by platform: Windows 95 and Macintosh.

Adding the Acrobat Distiller PPD with the Adobe driver (Windows 95)

1 Launch the setup utility for Adobe PostScript Printer Driver from the Drivers folder on the Acrobat 3.0 CD-ROM.

2 Follow the instructions on-screen to progress through the introduction, accept the license agreement, and copy the setup program to your local disk.

3 Choose Local Printer as your printer type, and click Next.

4 Locate the acrobat3/distillr/xtras folder, choose Acrobat Distiller from the list of available PPDs, and click Next.

5 Select FILE: from the list of available ports, and click Next.

6 Choose not to install this printer as the default printer or print a test page, and click Next.

7 Click OK to accept the Acrobat Distiller PPD properties.

8 Click Exit to exit the setup utility.

9 Select Settings > Printers from the Start menu, right-click the Acrobat Distiller printer, and select Properties.

10 Click the Fonts tab, then click the Send Fonts As button.

11 Select Outlines from the Send TrueType Fonts As: menu.

12 Enter 1 in the Threshold to switch between downloading bitmap or outline fonts… box, and click OK.

Note: Entering this value ensures that TrueType fonts will not be converted to Type 3 fonts in a PostScript file. Type 3 fonts can be the cause of unnecessarily large, slow PDF files.

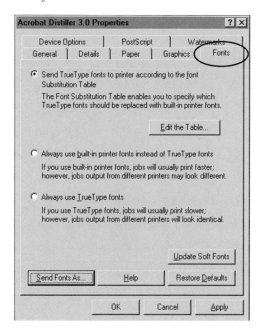

13 Click Apply to apply the changes.

14 Click OK to close the Acrobat Distiller Properties dialog box.

Adding the Acrobat Distiller PPD with the Adobe driver (Macintosh)

1 With PSPrinter 8.3.1 or later already installed, select the Chooser.

2 Click the PSPrinter icon. For Type, select Virtual Printer.

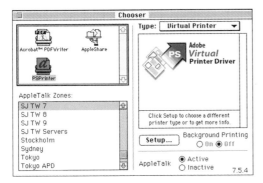

3 Click Setup. Navigate to System Folder: Extensions: Printer Descriptions, if you are not already there. Select Acrobat Distiller (PPD), and click Select.

4 Close the Chooser.

Now that you have set up the Adobe Acrobat Distiller PPD, you are ready to create a PostScript file and convert it to PDF with Acrobat Distiller.

Creating a PostScript file

In this section of the lesson, we suggest you open an existing document in your favorite application and loosely apply the steps that follow to create a PostScript file. Because Print dialog boxes can vary from application to application, it is difficult to provide you with specific instructions for creating a PostScript file from your favorite application. For specific instructions for creating a PostScript file from the application you are using, see the application's user manual.

After creating a PostScript file, follow the instructions for converting the PostScript file to PDF on page 59.

This section of the lesson is separated by platform: Windows 95, Windows NT 3.5.1 and Windows NT 4.0, and Macintosh.

To create a PostScript file (Windows 95):

1 Start your application, and open the document to be printed to a PostScript file.

2 Choose File > Print.

3 Select Acrobat Distiller from the printer list, and click OK.

4 Enter **Test.ps** as the filename for the PostScript file, save it in the PROJECTS folder, select All Files (*.*) from the Save As Type menu, and click OK.

Note: Some applications insist on using a .prn extension instead of the .ps extension that you designate. If this happens, you should rename the file with a .ps extension to allow Distiller to recognize and process the file.

To create a PostScript file in Windows NT:

You can use the Microsoft driver to create PostScript files in Windows NT 3.5.1 and 4.0. Contact your system administrator for assistance with setting up a PostScript printer driver to print to file. You should set up a PostScript printer with color capabilities such as an imagesetter.

Once you have a PostScript printer driver set up to print to file, choose that printer driver from the standard Print command in any application to create a PostScript file.

To create a PostScript file (Macintosh):

1 Start your application, and open the document to be printed to a PostScript file.

2 Select the Chooser.

3 Click the PSPrinter icon. Choose the printer you set up with the Acrobat Distiller PPD. Close the Chooser.

4 Return to your application.

5 Choose File > Print.

6 Select File as the destination if it is not already chosen. If the document is a color document or contains grayscale images, select the Color/Grayscale print option. (If you are using PSPrinter, click Options to set the Color/Grayscale Print option.)

7 Click Save or OK; the Save As dialog box appears.

8 Enter **Test.ps** as the filename, and save it in the PROJECTS folder.

9 Select the Binary and Level 2 Only buttons. Selecting these buttons creates the smallest and most efficient PostScript file.

10 Select All But Standard 13 from the Font Inclusion menu. Any TrueType and PostScript fonts used in the original document are included in the file.

11 Click Save. The PostScript file is created, and you are returned to your application.

Converting to PDF with Distiller

1 Start Acrobat Distiller.

2 Choose File > Open. Locate and select **Test.ps** from the list of files in the PROJECTS folder, and click Open.

3 Enter **Test.ps** as the filename, and save it in the PROJECTS folder. Distiller converts the file and outputs a PDF file to your PROJECTS folder.

4 Click OK.

5 Exit or Quit Distiller.

Take a moment to open the PDF file in Exchange and compare the display of the file to that of the original file. Compare the file size of the original document and the PDF file. You will find that the display of the PDF file closely matches the original, and in most cases, the PDF file size is significantly smaller than the original file size.

Creating a PDF file from Adobe PageMaker with Distiller

We have supplied a file and instructions for creating a PDF file from Adobe Page-Maker 6.5 with Distiller. If you do not have PageMaker 6.5, you can still read through the steps to familiarize yourself with the process. For specific instructions about creating PDF files from the applications you use, consult the application's user manual or the *Distiller Online Guide*.

Creating a PDF file with Distiller from PageMaker is a two-step process that can be streamlined to one step if you have approximately 24 MB of application RAM available. PageMaker comes with a plug-in, an extra piece of software, that allows PageMaker to communicate directly with Distiller to create a PDF file. You can use Distiller Assistant with other applications to communicate with Distiller directly as well. See the *Distiller Online Guide* for information about Distiller Assistant.

1 Start Adobe PageMaker.

2 Choose File > Open, then locate and select Flyerpc.p65 (Windows) or Flyermac.p65 (Macintosh) in the Lesson03 folder. If you receive a message indicating that the necessary fonts are not installed, see "Install the Classroom in a Book Fonts" on page 5, and install the fonts from the Classroom in a Book CD-ROM.

3 Choose File > Save As. Enter **Flyera.p65** as the filename and save it in your PROJECTS folder.

If you have approximately 24 MB of RAM, then you should complete steps 4-7. If you have less than 24 MB of RAM, skip to the "Creating a PDF file in two steps" section on page 70.

4 Choose File > Export > Adobe PDF.

5 Accept the default settings in the Export Adobe PDF dialog box, and click Export.

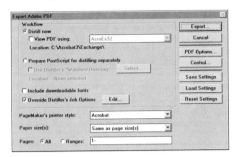

Windows dialog box   *Macintosh dialog box*

For most files, the default compression options create a quality PDF file. For a description of all the options available in the Export Adobe PDF dialog box, see the *PageMaker User Guide.* If you need to change the default options for your own files, follow the instructions in the PageMaker or Distiller guides.

To view an example of the results of choosing the various compression options, see the "Distributing PDF Documents" project on page 267.

6 Enter **Flyera.pdf** as the filename, save it in the PROJECTS folder, and click Save.

Distiller starts, the file is processed, and is saved as flyera.pdf in the PROJECTS folder.

You can use the one-step method to create PDF files with Distiller from other applications by using Distiller Assistant. See the *Distiller Online Guide* for information.

7 Exit or quit PageMaker and Distiller.

Viewing the PDF file

1 Start Acrobat Exchange.

2 Choose File > Open. Locate and select flyera.pdf in the PROJECTS folder, and click Open.

Take a moment to notice that Distiller has faithfully reproduced the original document in PDF. After viewing the PDF document, you can decide if you want to try the two-step method of creating a PDF document from PageMaker 6.5 in the next section or skip to the "Review" section on page 72.

3 Exit or quit Exchange.

Creating a PDF file in two steps

If you do not have enough RAM to run PageMaker and Distiller simultaneously, you need to create a PostScript file from PageMaker and then convert it to PDF in a separate step with Distiller.

A PostScript file contains a page description of the original file that Distiller uses to create the PDF file. By using this page description, Distiller produces a PDF file that maintains the original formatting, layout, and fonts used in the PageMaker file, just as a PostScript printer faithfully reproduces an electronic document on a printed page.

Creating a PostScript file

1 With the Flyerpc.p65 (Windows) or Flyermac.p65 (Macintosh) file open in PageMaker, choose File > Print.

2 For PPD, select Acrobat Distiller 2017.801 (Windows) or Acrobat Distiller (PPD) (Macintosh).

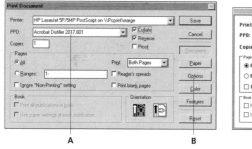 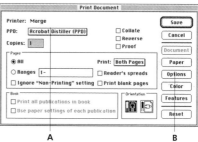

A   B   A   B

A. PPD B. Options

3 Click Options.

4 Select Write PostScript to file, and enter **Flyerb.pdf** as the filename.

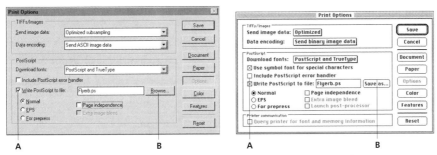

A. Write PostScript to File B. Browse (Windows), Save As (Macintosh)

5 Click Browse (Windows) or Save As (Macintosh), locate and open the PROJECTS folder, and click Save (Windows) or OK (Macintosh).

6 Click Save in the Print Options dialog box. The PostScript file is saved in the PROJECTS folder.

7 Exit or quit PageMaker. Do not save any changes to the file.

Converting to PDF

1 Start Distiller.

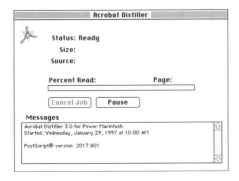

2 Choose File > Open. Locate and select Flyerb.ps from the list of files in the PROJECTS folder, and click Open.

3 Enter **Flyerb.pdf** as the filename, save it in the PROJECTS folder, and click OK. Distiller converts the file and outputs a PDF file to your PROJECTS folder.

4 Exit or quit Distiller.

Viewing the PDF file

Now take a look at the PDF document created by Distiller.

1 Start Acrobat Exchange.

2 Choose File > Open. Locate and select Flyerb.pdf from the list of files in the PROJECTS folder, and click Open.

As you can see, Distiller created an exact duplicate of the original file.

3 Exit or quit Exchange.

Review

In this lesson, you learned how to create PDF files from electronic documents with Acrobat Distiller and PDF Writer. In the following lessons, you will learn more about electronic publishing and how to enhance your PDF documents to make them interactive and easier to navigate.

To test your knowledge of the concepts and techniques you learned in this lesson, answer the following questions:

• Why should you use the Acrobat Distiller PPD when creating a PostScript file that will be processed by Acrobat Distiller?

• If your documents contain placed EPS images, which PDF creator should you use to create a PDF file?

• What are the advantages of using Distiller to create PDF files instead of PDF Writer?

• What are the advantages of using PDF Writer to create PDF files instead of Distiller?

• Why is it important to enter information in the Document Info fields?

• How would you create a PostScript file from your favorite application?

• Why are there a one-step method and a two-step method to creating PDF files with Distiller?

4

Lesson 4

Electronic Publishing with Adobe Acrobat

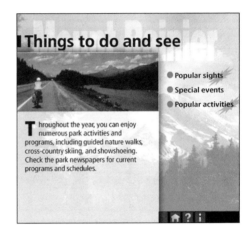

The desktop publishing revolution put quality publishing tools within reach of more people than ever before. Now easy access to the Internet and to CD-ROM recorders enables wider distribution of electronic publications— easily transportable documents that include links, sound, and video. The key to successful electronic publishing is the same as with paper publishing: understanding the requirements of the publication, the audience, and the distribution medium.

In this lesson, you'll learn how to do the following:

• Understand the different uses of print-on-demand electronic documents and documents designed for online use.

• Identify the software tools you need to create your electronic publication.

• Understand how PDF and HTML documents relate to each other.

• Identify the types of formatting and design decisions you need to make when creating an electronic publication.

This lesson will take about 35 minutes to complete.

On-screen viewing versus printing on demand

What does electronic publishing mean for your publication? Does it mean converting existing printed documents as is to an electronic format? Providing quick access to reference information? Or creating a full-fledged multimedia presentation? And perhaps most important, how will the publication be distributed and to what types of computer systems?

In this part of the lesson, you'll take a look at a number of electronic document samples.

1 Start Acrobat Exchange.

2 Choose File > Open. Select the Introduc.pdf file, located in the Lesson04 folder, and click Open. If needed, adjust the page magnification or use the scroll bars to bring the bottom part of the page into view.

The document previews on this page are links to the corresponding electronic documents. The top three previews link to documents designed to be both distributed and viewed electronically; the bottom three previews link to documents intended to be circulated online but printed out for viewing purposes.

3 Click the Schedule preview in the bottom row to open the corresponding PDF file.

This document is a work schedule that has been converted to PDF for easy electronic distribution.

4 Look at the page status bar at the bottom of the document window. Notice that the page size is a standard 8-1/2-by-11 inches, a suitable size for printing on a desktop printer.

You might glance at the schedule online, but you'd also want to print out a hard-copy version for handy reference.

5 Click the Go Back button (◀◀) in the toolbar to return to the previews.

Another example of a print-on-demand publication is the Documentation file: This text-intensive document is much easier to read in printed format rather than online format. If you want, click the Documentation preview in the bottom row to look at the file.

6 Click the Slide Show preview in the top row to open that document.

This document is a marketing presentation designed to be shown and viewed exclusively on-screen. Notice that the presentation opens in Full Screen mode to occupy all available space on the monitor.

7 Press Enter (Windows) or Return (Macintosh) several times to page through the presentation. Notice that the colorful graphics and page layout have been designed for optimal display on a monitor.

The Full Screen preference settings let you control how pages display in this mode. For example, you can have a full-screen document turn the page automatically after a certain number of seconds. For more information, see the *Exchange Online Guide.*

8 Press Esc to exit Full Screen mode.

9 Click the Go Back button(◀◀) until you return to the Introduc.pdf file.

An online help publication or an electronic catalog are further examples of documents for which on-screen viewing is suitable and even preferred. Electronic publishing offers intuitive navigational features, such as hypertext links, which are well suited for publications meant to be browsed or used as quick reference guides. If you want, click the previews in the top row to examine these documents.

10 Choose File > Close to close the Introduc.pdf document.

Electronic publishing tools

What tools do you need to publish electronically? The answer depends on what you want in your publication. In this part of the lesson, you'll open a document containing sample art that was created using a number of different software programs.

1 Choose File > Open. Select Tools.pdf, located in the Lesson04 folder, and click Open.

This page depicts a sample electronic document with different components of the document labelled according to the programs used to create them.

2 If needed, click the Fit Page button (▢) to view the entire page.

3 To find out more about an electronic publishing tool, click its label. To view information about the next or previous tool, click the arrows located in the bottom right corner of the page. To return to the overview page with the labelled document components, click the target icon located in the bottom right corner.

4 When you have finished viewing the document, choose File > Close to close it.

Publishing on the World Wide Web

The World Wide Web has greatly expanded the possibilities of bringing electronic documents to a wide and varied audience. With a Web browser, a user can read files that have been created using HTML (Hypertext Markup Language) and then posted on the Internet. However, because Web browsers can be configured to run other applications inside the browser window, you are not limited to viewing just HTML files. For example, you can post PDF files as part of a Web site; your users can then view these files right inside the browser window using Acrobat Reader.

Whether you should publish a document in HTML format or PDF depends on your document's needs. This section summarizes the different capabilities of HTML and PDF documents and provides some guidelines to help you determine which format to use.

About HTML

HTML is the native file format of the World Wide Web—that is, Web browsers read HTML pages directly, without any additional software. Properties of HTML documents include the following:

• When you create an HTML document, you format each page element—such as a heading or paragraph—by assigning a tag or identifier to it.

• A Web browser displays HTML documents dynamically, using whatever fonts and window size the user has specified for the browser on their computer. The same HTML page may have different appearances on different computers, depending on the browser settings on each computer.

• You can use other types of files in conjunction with HTML to enrich the content of your Web page. For example, you can place a graphics file or a movie clip in an HTML page so that users with the appropriate software and a properly configured browser can view and play multimedia elements live on the Web page.

About PDF

PDF is a cross-platform format that is transportable and viewable on any type of computer system—Windows, Macintosh, UNIX®, or OS/2. Users need a viewer such as Acrobat Reader or Exchange to view a PDF document. When including a

PDF file as part of your Web page, you should direct your users to the Adobe Systems Web page, from which they can download Reader free of charge (see page 10). Properties of PDF include the following:

• PDF preserves the exact layout, font attributes, and text formatting of electronic documents, regardless of the computer system or platform used to view these documents. As a result, publishing a Web page in PDF ensures that the page always appears in its original format and design.

• You can incorporate both text and graphics, as well as dynamic media such as sounds and movies into a PDF file. You can also add interactive features such as hyperlinks and form fields.

• PDF documents can be viewed one page at a time and printed from the Web. With page-at-a-time downloading, the Web server sends only the requested page to the user, thus decreasing downloading time. In addition, the user can easily print selected pages or all pages from the document. PDF is a suitable format for publishing long electronic documents on the Web.

• You can use security passwords to lock your PDF documents from undesired changes or to limit access to important documents. Password protection provides you with an extra measure of security when publishing over the Internet. Lesson 10 covers document security in detail.

• Users can change the view magnification of a PDF page using controls in Acrobat Reader. This feature can be especially useful for zooming in on graphics or diagrams containing intricate details.

• You can use a Web search engine to index PDF documents for rapid searching on the Web.

Comparing an HTML and a PDF document

To illustrate the differences between HTML and PDF document features, you will watch a movie comparing these two types of documents.

1 Choose File > Open. Select the Mov_page.pdf file, located in the Lesson04 folder, and click Open.

2 Click the Play Movie button in the page to view the movie. When you are finished, close the Mov_page.pdf file.

Making document design decisions

Once you have identified the audience for your publication, you can begin to make the formatting and production decisions that will help make the publication attractive and easy to use. If you're simply converting an existing paper document to electronic format, you'll inevitably weigh the benefits of reworking the design against the time and cost required to do so. If your publication will be viewed both on-screen and on paper, you may have to make the design accommodate the different requirements of on-screen viewing and paper output.

Print-on-demand documents

First you'll take a look at a document designed to be browsed online but printed out for closer viewing.

1 Choose File > Open. Select the Introduc.pdf file, located in the Lesson04 folder, and click Open.

2 Select the hand tool, and click the Brochure preview at the bottom of the page to open the corresponding document.

This document is a printed brochure that was converted as is to electronic format. Converting the document to PDF is a good way to distribute it cheaply and easily. It also enables you to use features such as hypertext links to make navigation of the brochure both easy and intuitive.

3 If needed, click the Fit Page button (▣) to view the entire page. Click the Next Page button (▶) in the toolbar a few times to page through the brochure.

Notice, however, that while the online brochure is useful for quick browsing and printing selected pages, it is not designed to be read on-screen. The long and narrow pages are inconveniently shaped for the screen, and the small image and type sizes make viewing a strain for the user.

Documents optimized for on-screen viewing

1 Click the Go Back button (◀◀) until you return to the Introduc.pdf file, and click the Interactive Brochure preview at the top of the page to open that document.

This document is the Mount Rainier brochure redesigned and optimized for online viewing. The topics in the brochure have been redesigned as a series of nested, linked topic screens that lead the reader through the document.

2 If needed, click the Fit Page button (▣) to view the entire page.

Notice that the horizontal page orientation is well suited for display on a monitor.

3 Click About the Park to activate that link.

The About the Park topic screen appears, with its own list of subtopics. Notice how the larger image and type sizes make this brochure easier to view than the print-on-demand version.

Notice also the use of sans serif fonts in the publication. Sans serif fonts have simpler and cleaner shapes than serif fonts, making them easier to read on-screen.

Serif font

Sans serif font

4 Click Flora & Fauna to jump to that topic screen. Then click Lowland Forest to view a specific information screen.

Notice that the pages of the brochure have been redesigned to accommodate a navigational structure based on self-contained, screen-sized units.

The formatting considerations of on-screen publications—fonts, page size, layout, color, resolution— are the same as those of other kinds of publications; however, each element must be reevaluated in the context of on-screen viewing. Decisions about issues such as color and resolution, which in traditional publishing may require a trade-off between quality and cost, may require a parallel trade-off between quality and file size in electronic publishing. Once you have determined the page elements that are important to you, you need to choose the publishing tools and format that will best maintain the desired elements. For more information on designing online publications, see the *Electronic Publishing Guide*, located on the Acrobat Classroom in a Book CD-ROM.

5 Choose File > Close to close the interactive brochure.

Review

In this lesson, you've examined a variety of electronic documents designed in different file formats for different purposes. Later on in this book, you'll get some hands-on practice in creating and tailoring your own electronic documents.

To test your knowledge of the concepts and techniques you learned in this lesson, answer the following questions:

• How do print-on-demand electronic documents differ from documents optimized for online use?

• What hardware and software do you need to view PDF documents?

• What kinds of media can you use to distribute PDF documents?

• What factors determine the layout and appearance of an HTML page? A PDF page?

• What kinds of typefaces and type sizes are best suited for on-screen display?

5

Lesson 5

Using and Creating Navigational Structures

Exchange includes several features that let you organize and navigate a document from an overview perspective. Bookmarks represent headings that link to their corresponding sections in the document; thumbnails let you preview the contents of and navigate each page; and articles let you follow a thread of information that spans more than one column on a page or across pages.

In this lesson, you'll learn how to do the following:

- Create bookmarks that link to specific views in a document.
- Use thumbnails to navigate through a document.
- Use thumbnails to change the magnification level and viewed area.
- Create a link that jumps to a different PDF document.
- Replace a PDF page with a page from a different PDF document.
- Follow an article thread.

This lesson will take about 35 minutes to complete.

Opening the work file

You'll start by opening an online newsletter published by a fictitious company called Juggler Toys.

1 Start Acrobat Exchange.

2 Choose File > Open.

3 Select News.pdf, located in the Lesson05 folder, and click Open.

Using bookmarks

A bookmark is a link represented by text in the overview window. Instead of creating a hot spot on the document page, you create a text list in the overview window that is linked to different views or pages in the document.

You can use electronic bookmarks as you would paper bookmarks, to mark a place in a document that you want to recall or return to later. You can also use bookmarks to create a brief custom outline of a document or to open other documents.

Looking at existing bookmarks

When bookmarks are displayed, they appear in an overview window to the left of the document. To maximize the screen area used for display, the Juggler Toys newsletter is set to open with the overview window closed. You use the Bookmarks and Page button in the toolbar to display bookmarks.

1 Click the Bookmarks and Page button (▦).

A list of bookmarks representing stories in the newsletter appears. You may not be able to read all of the bookmark text on your screen. You'll resize the overview window to display the bookmarks completely.

2 Adjust the width of the overview window by dragging the resize box at the lower right corner of the window.

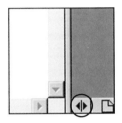 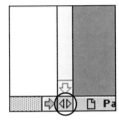

Resize box in
Windows

Resize box on the
Macintosh

3 Click the text of the Q & A bookmark to go to the page where the corresponding story appears. Be sure to click the bookmark text, and not the page icon to the left of the text.

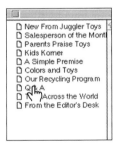

You should be on page 3 viewing the Q & A topic.

Adding bookmarks

The current bookmark list lacks a few needed entries. You'll add some of the missing bookmarks to the list.

1 Click the Kids Korner bookmark to go to the corresponding topic on page 2.

2 Scroll up to bring the "Family Night Focus" topic into view.

Notice that the "Family Night Focus" topic does not have a corresponding bookmark in the overview window. You will add a Family Night Focus bookmark to the list.

3 Click the select-text tool (⬚abc⬚).

4 Move the pointer into the page, and drag to highlight the title "Family Night Focus."

Family Night Focus

The Theme of October's Family Night will be "Flying Objects." Three teams will present their prototypes for testing to the Juggler Toys community. Here are a few hints about what's in store: flying saucers, self-propelling creatures, and other airborne objects. (Okay, now *you* guess.)

As always, we encourage you to bring your children. They're always our best critics. Dining will begin at 6 ᴾᴹ, and Show-and-Test will begin around 8 ᴾᴹ. Wear comfortable clothes and bring a dish to share. Beverages and dessert will be provided. We'll look forward to seeing you there!

If you have trouble highlighting just the title, hold down Ctrl (Windows) or Option (Macintosh) and drag a marquee around the title text.

5 Choose Document > New Bookmark to create a new bookmark with the highlighted text as its title.

A Family Night Focus bookmark appears at the bottom of the bookmark list. If no bookmarks are selected when you create a new bookmark, the new bookmark appears at the end of the list.

By default, the new bookmark links to the current page view displayed on your screen.

6 Click in the blank area in the overview window to deselect all bookmarks. Then click the First Page button (◀) to go to the start of the newsletter.

7 Click the hand tool, and click the text of the Family Night Focus bookmark to jump to its corresponding story.

Moving a bookmark

After creating a bookmark, you can move it to its proper place in the list. You reorder bookmarks by dragging them.

1 Click the page icon for the Family Night Focus bookmark to select the bookmark.

Clicking the page icon for a bookmark selects that bookmark for editing; clicking the text of a bookmark activates the bookmark's link.

2 Drag the page icon up until a black bar appears under the page icon for the Parents Praise Toys bookmark.

The black bar indicates the new location for the selected bookmark.

3 Release the mouse to reorder the bookmark.

4 Click in the overview window to deselect the bookmarks.

Setting bookmark destinations

Bookmark destinations default to the view you are looking at when you create a bookmark. Although you can set bookmark destinations as you create each bookmark, it is sometimes easier to create a group of bookmarks, and set the destinations later. For example, if you are creating a table of contents, you can create the bookmark list first, and then page through the document to add the destinations.

In this section, you will add the bookmarks for the pictures and advertisements in this newsletter. You will add three bookmarks and then set their destinations.

1 Click the page icon for the New From Juggler Toys bookmark to select it.

2 Choose Document > New Bookmark. A new untitled bookmark appears below the previously selected bookmark.

3 Type **Pictures & Ads** as the bookmark title.

4 Choose Document > New Bookmark to create another untitled bookmark, and type **Galaxy Guy** as the name.

5 Choose Document > New Bookmark, and name the bookmark **Retro Toys Ad**.

6 Click in the blank area of the overview window to deselect all bookmarks.

7 Use the hand tool to test out your new bookmarks.

Notice that the bookmarks all link by default to the current page view. Next, you'll reset the destinations for the Galaxy Guy and Retro Toys Ad bookmarks.

8 Click the First Page button (◀), and click the Fit Page button (▣) to view page 1 in its entirety.

9 Click the zoom tool (⊕), and marquee zoom around the Galaxy Guy picture.

10 Click the page icon for the Galaxy Guy bookmark to highlight it for editing; then choose Document > Reset Bookmark Destination to reset the destination to the view currently displayed on-screen. Click Yes to confirm resetting the bookmark destination.

11 Go to page 3, click the Fit Page button (▣), and use the zoom tool to marquee zoom around the Retro Toys advertisement at the bottom of the page.

12 Click the page icon for the Retro Toys Ad bookmark to select it, choose Document > Reset Bookmark Destination, and click Yes to the message.

Instead of assigning a view destination for the Pictures & Ads bookmark, you'll make the bookmark into a placeholder heading for the Galaxy Guy and Retro Toys bookmarks.

13 Click the page icon for the Pictures & Ads bookmark, and choose Edit > Properties.

14 For Type, choose None, and click Set Action.

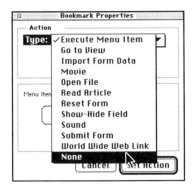

The default bookmark action is to link to a page view. Choosing None as the action type means that the Pictures & Ads bookmark does not link to any destination and acts solely as a placeholder.

15 Click in the overview window to deselect the bookmarks.

16 Select the hand tool and try out your bookmarks. Notice that the Pictures & Ads bookmark does not change the page view.

Nesting bookmarks

Bookmarks can be used to create a hierarchical outline of a document, with several bookmarks nested under a common heading. In this section, you will nest the Galaxy Guy and Retro Toys Ad bookmarks under the Pictures & Ads bookmark.

1 Click the page icon for the Galaxy Guy bookmark.

2 Hold down Shift, and click the page icon for the Retro Toys Ad bookmark to add it to the selection. Release the Shift key.

3 Position the pointer over the page icon for the Galaxy Guy bookmark.

4 Hold down the mouse button and drag up and to the right until the black bar is under the "P" in Pictures & Ads.

5 Release the mouse button.

The selected bookmarks appear as sub-bookmarks under the Pictures & Ads heading.

You've just learned how to create, move, and assign actions to bookmarks. In later lessons, you'll learn how to create bookmarks that play other actions such as movies or sounds.

Using thumbnails

Thumbnails are miniature previews of your document pages. Like bookmarks, thumbnails appear in the overview window to the left of the document.

In this part of the lesson, you'll use thumbnails to navigate and change the view of pages in the newsletter. Later on in this book you'll learn how to use thumbnails to reorder pages in a document.

1 Click the First Page button (◀) to return to the start of the newsletter. Click the Actual Page button (◻) to view the page at 100% magnification.

2 Click the Thumbnails and Page button (▦). Notice that gray thumbnail place-holders appear for each page in the document window. You'll generate the actual thumbnails in the next step.

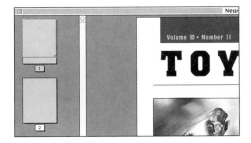

Because thumbnails take up extra file space (about 3K per thumbnail), they are not automatically created with a document.

3 Choose Document > Create All Thumbnails.

Thumbnails for every page in the document are created. You can cancel thumbnail generation at any time by clicking Cancel (Windows) or pressing Command-period (Macintosh). The thumbnails created before you canceled will appear in the overview window.

4 If the thumbnails are not all visible in the overview window, use the scroll bar to scroll through the thumbnails.

Notice that the thumbnails represent both the content and the page orientation of the pages in the newsletter. Page-number boxes appear below each thumbnail.

5 Click the page 3 thumbnail to go to that page. Be sure to click the thumbnail image, not the page-number box.

The page number for the thumbnail becomes highlighted, and a 100% view of page 3 appears in the document window, centered on the point you clicked.

Take a look at the page 3 thumbnail. The dotted grey rectangle inside the thumbnail represents the area contained by the current page view. You can use this view box to adjust the area and magnification being viewed.

6 Position the pointer over the lower right corner of the view box; the pointer turns into a double-headed arrow.

7 Drag upward to shrink the view box and release the mouse button. Take a look at the status bar and notice that the magnification level has increased to accommodate the smaller area being viewed.

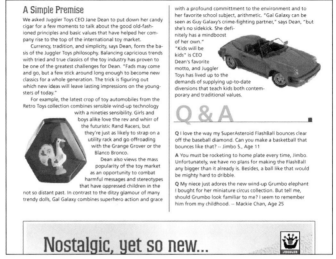

Place pointer over lower right corner of view box...

Document view

and drag up to increase magnification.

Resulting view

A Simple Premise

We asked Juggler Toys CEO Jane Dean to put down her candy cigar for a few moments to talk about the good old-fashioned principles and basic values that have helped her company rise to the top of the international toy market.

Currency, tradition, and simplicity, says Dean, form the basis of the Juggler Toys philosophy. Balancing capricious trends with tried and true classics of the toy industry has proven to be one of the greatest challenges for Dean. "Fads may come and go, but a few stick around long enough to become new classics for a whole generation. The trick is figuring out which new ideas will leave lasting impressions on the youngsters of today."

For example, the latest crop of toy automobiles from the Retro Toys collection combines sensible wind-up technology

8 Now move your pointer inside the view box. Notice that the pointer changes to a hand.

9 Drag the view box within the thumbnail and watch the view change in the document window when you release the mouse button.

View box   *Document view*

View box dragged   *Resulting view*
downward

10 Drag the view box down to focus your view on the ad at the bottom of this page.

Thumbnails provide a convenient way to monitor and adjust your page view in a document.

11 Click the Page Only button (▣) to close the thumbnail overview window.

Creating a cross-document link

In Lesson 2, you learned how to create links to different page views and Web sites. Now you'll learn how to create a link that jumps to a different PDF document.

In addition to the toy newsletter, Juggler Toys publishes a variety of documents to help advertise, catalog, and sell its products. You'll create a link from the Retro Toys ad in this newsletter to an online brochure detailing the Retro Toys collection.

1 Click the Fit Page button(▣).

2 Click the link tool (✎), and drag a marquee that surrounds the Retro Toys ad.

3 Under Appearance, for Type, choose Invisible Rectangle.

In addition to setting the appearance of a link's border, you can also specify the highlight appearance of a link when it is clicked.

4 For Highlight, choose Outline.

The Outline option displays the link as a black rectangle when clicked. The following illustration shows the different highlight appearances available in Exchange.

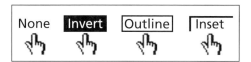

5 Under Action, for Type, choose Go to View.

In Acrobat, a view consists of a specific PDF page and magnification; the page can be part of the current document, or it can be part of an entirely different PDF document.

6 From the menu bar, choose File > Open. Select Brochure.pdf, located in the Lesson05 folder, and click Open.

7 In the Create Link window, for magnification, choose Fit Page to display the full brochure page when the link is activated.

8 Click Set Link.

9 Click the hand tool, and test the link you've created.

10 Click the Go Back button (◀◀) to retrace the link back to the original document and view.

Replacing a page

Sometimes you may want to replace an entire PDF page with another PDF page. For example, if you want to change the design or layout of a PDF page, you can revise the source page in your original design application, convert the modified page to PDF, and use it to replace the old PDF page. When you replace a page, only the text and graphics on the original page are replaced. The replacement does not affect any interactive elements associated with the original page, such as links or bookmarks.

In this part of the lesson, you'll replace page 3 of the newsletter with a page that contains a new version of the Retro Toys ad, and observe what happens to the link you just created around the ad.

1 Choose Document > Replace Pages.

2 Select Newspage.pdf, located in the Lesson05 folder, and click Select.

3 In the Replace Pages dialog box, make sure you are replacing page 3 to 3 of the News.pdf with page 1 to 1 of Newspage.pdf, and click OK.

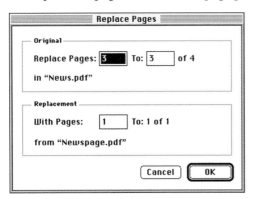

Exchange replaces the page with the revised page from the Newspage.pdf document. Now you'll verify that the original ad link is still in place.

Click the Fit Page button (▢). Then click the zoom tool(🔍) and marquee-zoom around the revised ad at the bottom of the page.

Notice the different graphics used in the new ad.

4 Click the hand tool, and click the ad to jump to the brochure. Click Go Back (◀) to return to the newsletter.

You can think of PDF links as existing in their own layer on top of pages in a document. Links are not inherently tied to graphic or text elements in a document. When you replace, insert, or extract pages from a document, the links remain unaffected and maintain their relative positions and sizes in their link layer.

Because the Retro Toys ad in your replacement page has the same size and position as the ad in the original page, the cross-document link you created still references the correct part of the new page. However, if your replacement page contains shifted graphics and text blocks, you may have to move your links to correct their positions. For more information on preserving and adjusting links when you revise a document, see page 32 of the *Electronic Publishing Guide,* located on the Acrobat Classroom in a Book CD-ROM.

Using articles

Although the Juggler Toys newsletter has been converted to an online format, it still uses a layout associated with printed newsletters. The restrictions of the screen can make the reading of some documents quite difficult. For example, documents created in a column format can be particularly difficult to follow.

Acrobat's article feature lets you guide users through material that lies in columns or across a series of nonconsecutive pages. You use the article tool to create a series of linked rectangles that connect the separate sections of the material and follow the flow of text. You can also generate article threads automatically from a page layout file as you distill it (see "Automatically generating links and bookmarks" on page 115).

In this part of the lesson, you'll examine an article that has already been created. You'll learn how to create an article thread in the project, "Creating an Online Version of a Book," starting on page 137.

1 Choose View > Articles.

2 Select Colors and Toys, and click View.

The beginning of the "Colors and Toys" article on page 2 appears.

3 Move your pointer on top of the article. The downward pointing arrow inside the hand pointer indicates that you are following an article thread.

> ### Colors and Toys
>
> Even superheroes can use a fashion lift sometimes. "I stumbled through the universe with the same flash sky boots and aquamarine torpedo pack for I don't know how many eons," says Gal Galaxy, the crime-busting heroine and be-loved space icon. "Baby blue was cramping my style. I needed a change." Well, thanks to the world-renowned color special-ists at Juggler Toys Company, Gal Galaxy can wash her blues away. This fall season finds our intrepid interstellar cadet decked out in brand new acid-washed rocket overalls avail-able in a variety of colors, including Asteroid Belt Sunrise, Cosmic Marine, Martian Rust, and Plutonium Peach. Exclaims the seasonal action figure, "My awesome new threads have put a spring in my step and a wallop in my rocket booster.

4 Press Enter (Windows) or Return (Macintosh) to advance to the next section of the article that will fit on your screen.

5 Hold down Shift.

Notice that the arrow in the hand pointer now points upward. You hold down Shift to reverse your direction in an article.

> ists at Juggler Toys Company, Gal Galaxy can wash her blues away. This fall season finds our intrepid interstellar cadet decked out in brand new acid-washed rocket overalls avail-able in a variety of colors, including Asteroid Belt Sunrise, Cosmic Marine, Martian Rust, and Plutonium Peach. Exclaims the seasonal action figure, "My awesome new threads have put a spring in my step and a wallop in my rocket booster. I've mopped up three toxic spills, rounded up four runaway satellites, and reversed the greenhouse effect on two planets already. And that's just today."
>
> With her newly expanded wardrobe, Gal Galaxy can look forward to a fresh change of costume after every adventure. (Continued on p4)

6 While holding down Shift, press Enter or Return. Then release Shift.

You are moved back one view along the article thread.

7 Now resume your advance through the article by pressing Enter or Return. Keep advancing until you reach the text that reads "Continued on p.4."

Look at the status bar and notice that you are currently on page 2.

8 Press Enter or Return.

Look at the page number in the status bar. You have advanced from page 2 to page 4 to follow the article.

You can exit article mode at any time by choosing any navigational method not associated with articles.

9 Click the Fit Page button(◻) to exit the article.

10 Click the zoom tool (🔍), and marquee-drag around the text under the elephant image in the left column.

11 Click the hand tool, and move the pointer over the parenthesized text that says "Colors and Toys continued." A downward arrow with a bar above it appears inside the hand pointer, indicating that the text beneath is part of an article thread.

A Mackie, your memory serves you well. The Grumbo wind-up toy was inspired by Grumbo the Great, the legendary gymnastic elephant who travelled with the Dingaling Brothers Circus about twenty years ago. Grumbo the Great has long since passed on to that great savannah in the sky, but Grumbo wind-up reminds us daily of those amazing feats and death-defying stunts of yore.

(Colors and Toys continued)
But unlike such glam-queens as Kiddie Karol or the infamous Bimbi, Gal Galaxy is not about to fall into the valley of the dolls. "I won't let this new mood makeover get to my head. All my outfits value function over fashion - after all, I'm much more than just a pretty pair of boots." Nevertheless, Gal Galaxy continues to set the standard for interstellar chic. Says Guy Galaxy, who's scheduled to have his colors re-evaluated next year, "Gal's new look is fabulous - it says 'high style' and 'environment' all at once."

12 Click the text to enter the article thread. Notice that you enter the article at the section you clicked.

You can return to the beginning of an article at any time.

13 Hold down Ctrl (Windows) or Option (Macintosh) so that an upward arrow with a bar above it appears in the hand pointer. Click inside the article to go to the start of the article.

(Colors and Toys continued)
But unlike such glam-queens as Kiddie Karol or the infamous Bimbi, Gal Galaxy is not about to fall into the valley of the dolls. "I won't let this new mood makeover get to my head. All my outfits value function over fashion - after all, I'm much more than just a pretty pair of boots." Nevertheless, Gal Galaxy continues to set the standard for interstellar chic. Says Guy Galaxy, who's scheduled to have his colors re-evaluated next year, "Gal's new look is fabulous - it says 'high style' and 'environment' all at once."

Our Recycling Program
The response has been overwhelming. Since we announced

Here, you first entered the article at its middle section and then used the Ctrl or Option key to jump to the article's beginning. You can also enter an article automatically at its beginning point by holding down Ctrl or Option and clicking any section of the article.

14 Press Enter or Return to advance through the article. When you reach the end of the article, a bar appears below the arrow in the hand pointer.

15 Click the Actual Page button(◻) to exit the article thread.

16 Choose File > Save As, name the document 05work.pdf, and save it in your PROJECTS folder.

17 Close all documents.

Review

In this lesson, you've learned how to use bookmarks and thumbnails to make navigation of your document easier. In later lessons, you'll learn how to assign actions to bookmarks and change page order using thumbnails.

To test your knowledge of the concepts and techniques you learned in this lesson, answer the following questions:

• What happens when you click the text of a bookmark? What happens when you click the page icon for a bookmark?

• How do you change your viewed area or magnification using thumbnails?

• Name two ways in which you can enter an article thread.

• Can you assign an action to a thumbnail?

• If you replace a page with links on it, what happens to the links after the replacement?

6

Lesson 6

Modifying PDF Documents

Once you've converted your document to PDF, you can use Acrobat Exchange to make final edits and modifications. In addition to adding links and bookmarks to a document, you can edit text and insert, reorder, and extract pages.

In this lesson, you'll learn how to do the following:

- Import a TIFF image file (Windows only).

- Rotate and crop pages.

- Use thumbnails to rearrange pages in a document.

- Insert and extract pages from a document.

- Edit and change the appearance of text in a document.

- Create links and bookmarks that play actions.

This lesson will take about 45 minutes to complete.

Opening and examining the work file

You'll work with an edition of *Aesop's Fables* that has been designed for online view-ing and converted to PDF. Because this online book has passed through multiple designers and design cycles, it contains a number of mistakes. In this lesson, you'll use Exchange to correct the problems in this PDF document and optimize *Aesop's Fables* for the next generation of wise youngsters.

1 Start Acrobat Exchange.

2 Choose File > Open.

3 Select Afables.pdf, located in the Lesson06 folder, and click Open.

Notice that bookmarks for the individual fables have already been created.

4 Select the hand tool, and click the Table of Contents bookmark to go to the table of contents.

5 Move the pointer into the document. Notice that the titles in the list have already been linked.

6 Click The Fox and the Grapes to follow its link. Click the Go Back button (◀◀) to return to the table of contents.

Automatically generating links and bookmarks

Certain page layout and book publishing programs, such as Adobe PageMaker or Adobe FrameMaker, work in conjunction with Acrobat Distiller to automate the creation of PDF link features during the distilling process. For example, this edition of *Aesop's Fables* was originally designed using PageMaker. When the PageMaker file was distilled to PDF, the entries in the formatted table of contents were converted to PDF bookmarks and links automatically.

AUTOMATICALLY CREATING LINKS, BOOKMARKS, AND ARTICLES You can generate PDF links, bookmarks, and articles from a FrameMaker or PageMaker file by properly formatting corresponding elements in the original file. Tables of contents and paragraph headings convert to linked lists of contents and bookmarks in PDF; cross-references convert to links; and connected text frames convert to article threads. For detailed information, see your FrameMaker or PageMaker documentation.

1. *Create cross-references and table of contents in FrameMaker and PageMaker.*

2. *Create text frames to preserve text flow.*

3. *In FrameMaker, choose File > Print, select Generate Acrobat Data, click Acrobat Setup, and specify the paragraph tags you want to convert to bookmarks. In PageMaker, choose File > Create Adobe PDF, click PDF options, and select Link TOC entries and Create Bookmarks.*

4. *Distill file to PDF.*

5. *Open PDF file in Exchange, and examine the generated links, bookmarks, and articles.*

Editing pages

Take a few moments to page through *Aesop's Fables.* Go to the first page of the document and notice that the book has no title page. We've created a separate title page for you by scanning a printed image into a computer and saving the image as a TIFF file.

If you are using Acrobat for Windows, you will use the Import plug-in to import the TIFF image as a title page and edit the page to fit the rest of the book. If you are using a Macintosh, you will insert a version of the title page that has already been converted to PDF. (At the time of publication, the Import plug-in was only available for the Windows 95 and Windows NT 3.5.1 versions of Acrobat 3.0.)

Importing an image (Windows only)

1 Choose File > Import > Image.

2 Select Cover.tif, located in the Lesson06 folder, and click Open.

The Import Image dialog box appears.

3 Select Append Images to Current Document, and click OK.

The cover image is appended to the end of the document. The imported page is converted to PDF Image Only mode, meaning that the bitmap images and text in the page are pictures that cannot be edited in Exchange. For more information on how and what types of image formats Exchange can import, see the *Exchange Online Guide.*

4 Proceed to "Rotating a page" on page 117.

Inserting the title page (Macintosh only)

Perform the following procedure if you are using a Macintosh version of Acrobat without the Capture plug-in.

1 Choose Document > Insert Pages. Select the Cover.pdf file, located in the Lesson06 folder, and click Select.

2 For Location, click After; for Page, click Last. Then click OK.

The Cover.pdf file represents a version of the TIFF title page that has already been converted to PDF. Now that you've inserted the title page to your document, you can proceed to the next section, "Rotating a page."

Rotating a page

Now that you've imported or inserted the new title page, you'll rotate it so that it's oriented correctly on your screen.

1 Click the Fit Page button (⬜) to view the whole page you imported. Notice that the page is oriented incorrectly—a problem that commonly occurs when scanning an image.

2 Choose Document > Rotate Pages.

The Rotate Pages dialog box lets you rotate one or more pages by 90 degrees in a specified direction.

3 For Direction, click Counterclockwise. For Pages, make sure that you are rotating just page 17 of the document.

4 Click OK. When the confirmation message appears, click OK to rotate the page.

5 Click the Thumbnails and Page button (▦), and scroll through the overview window to view the last thumbnail for the page you just rotated.

Although the thumbnail is gray, you can see that this page is larger than the other pages in the book. You'll crop the imported page to make it exactly the same size as the other pages.

Cropping a page

1 Choose Document > Crop Pages.

The Crop Pages dialog box appears, letting you specify the cropping margins in inches.

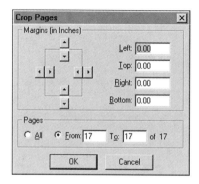

2 For Left, enter **2.1**. A dotted line representing the crop location appears in the document.

You may need to drag the Crop Pages dialog box out of the way to view the crop line properly.

3 Use the left pair of arrows in the Crop Pages dialog box to fine-tune the location of the crop line so that it aligns with the edge of the title border.

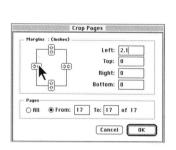

4 Press Tab to move to the number field for Top, and enter **1.5**.

5 Enter the following values for the remaining crop fields: **2.2** for Right and **1.6** for Bottom. (Press Tab to move from field to field.) Then use the arrows to fine-tune the crop lines.

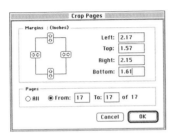

6 For Pages, make sure you are cropping just page 17 of the document.

7 Click OK. Click OK again to the confirmation message to crop the title page.

8 Choose File > Save As, name the document 06work.pdf, and save it in your PROJECTS folder.

Moving a page

Now that you've corrected the size and page orientation of the cover, you'll move it to the front of the book. You rearrange pages in a PDF document using thumbnails.

1 Choose Document > Create All Thumbnails to create the thumbnail for the imported page.

2 Drag the double-headed arrow at the bottom right corner of the overview window to enlarge the window. Resize the overview window so that you can view the thumbnails in two columns.

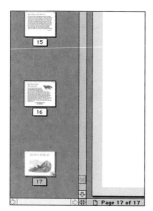 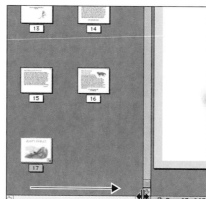

In addition to providing convenient previews of your pages, thumbnails let you change the placement of pages by dragging.

3 If needed, scroll through the thumbnails to view the page 17 thumbnail. Place your pointer over the page-number box for this thumbnail, and click. A black rectangle outlines the thumbnail, indicating that you can move the thumbnail.

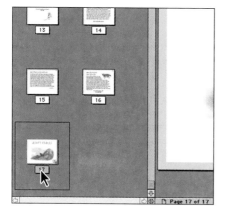

4 Drag the page-number box upward in the overview window to move the thumbnail (the window scrolls automatically). Drag upward until the black insertion bar appears to the left of the page 1 thumbnail, and release the mouse button.

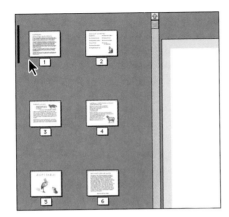

The cover page is repositioned in the document as page 1, and the remaining page numbers change accordingly.

Moving multiple pages

Next, you'll move two pages of a fable that have been placed in the wrong section of the book.

1 Click the page 3 thumbnail to go to the table of contents.

2 Click the Fit Width button (⬚) to display all of the contents.

3 Click "The Ant and the Grasshopper" to jump to that fable. Although this fable was listed last in the contents, it is not the last fable in the book.

4 Click the page-number box of the page 13 thumbnail to select the thumbnail. Hold down Shift and click the page-number box of the page 14 thumbnail to select it as well.

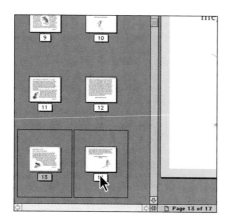

You hold down Shift while clicking to select multiple thumbnails.

5 Release the Shift key.

6 Position your pointer over the page-number box for the page 13 thumbnail, and hold down the mouse.

7 Drag down until the black insertion bar appears to the right of the page 17 thumbnail. Release the mouse to insert the thumbnails into their new position.

Inserting a single page

Next you'll insert a page from a different file to complete a fable in 06work.pdf. You use thumbnails to insert a single page into a document.

1 Resize the overview window to view the thumbnails in a single column.

2 Click the thumbnail for page 14. Then click the Fit Page button (□).

You are viewing "The Frog and the Ox." Notice that this fable is continued on another page.

3 Click the Next Page button.

Unfortunately, you can't read the end of the fable because it simply isn't there. You'll open up the PDF document that contains the missing page and insert the page into this file.

4 Choose File > Open. Select Frog_ox.pdf, located in the Lesson06 folder, and click Open.

5 Choose Window > Tile Vertically to arrange the two document windows side by side.

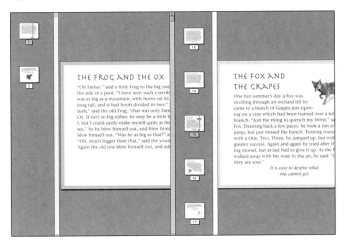

You can drag thumbnails between document windows to insert pages.

6 Click the page-number box for the page 2 Frog_ox.pdf thumbnail to select it.

7 Drag the selected thumbnail by its page-number box into the overview window for 06work.pdf. When the black bar appears between the page 14 and page 15 thumbnails, release the mouse button.

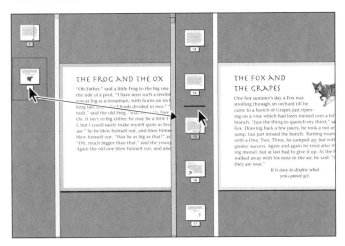

The second page of the fable becomes page 15 in the book.

8 Close Frog_ox.pdf, and resize the 06work.pdf window to fill your desktop.

9 Click the page 15 thumbnail to view your newly inserted page.

Inserting an entire file

In Exchange, you can insert a page, a specified range of pages, or all pages from one PDF document to another. In the previous section, you used thumbnails to insert a page from one PDF document to another. Now you'll add a fable to the 06work.pdf file by inserting all the pages from another file. You can insert an entire file easily by using the Insert Pages command.

1 Click the Bookmarks and Page button (⬛) to display the bookmarks in the overview window. If needed, resize the overview window to view the entire bookmark text.

The Lion's Share bookmark appears in the bookmark list, but the actual fable is missing from the book. You'll insert the missing fable from another document.

2 Use the scroll box in the scroll bar to go to page 9.

3 Choose Document > Insert Pages. Select Lions.pdf, located in the Lesson06 folder, and click Select.

The Insert dialog box appears.

4 For Location, click Before. For Page, click Page, make sure that **9** appears in the page field, and then click OK.

The fable entitled "The Lion's Share" is inserted in place.

5 Page through the document to verify that the fable has been inserted in the correct location. "The Lion's Share" should appear after "The Dog and the Shadow" and before "The Lion and the Mouse."

6 Choose File > Save As, and save 06work.pdf in your PROJECTS folder. You can replace the existing file.

Extracting a page

Now you'll remove an unneeded page from the document and save it as a separate PDF file.

1 Go to page 6, and notice that this page functions as a second title page.

Although a second title page might be appropriate for a printed book, it seems repetitive and unnecessary in an online document, where readers will most likely not flip through the pages in order.

2 Choose Document > Extract Pages.

3 Make sure you are extracting from page 6 to 6 of the document, and select Delete Pages After Extracting. Click OK. When the confirmation message appears, click OK again.

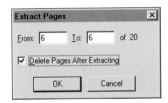

The title page is deleted from the 06work.pdf file and opened as a new one-page document.

4 Choose File > Save As. Name the document Title.pdf, and save it in your PROJECTS folder.

5 Close Title.pdf.

Notice that the extra title page has been deleted from the fables book.

Renumbering pages

You may have noticed that the page numbers on the document pages do not always match the page numbers that appear below the thumbnails and in the status bar. An Acrobat viewer always numbers pages with Arabic numerals, starting with page 1 for the first page in the document, and so on. Because the *Aesop's Fables* document contains front matter such as the copyright page and table of contents, its body pages do not follow the numbering shown in the status bar.

When you are preparing a document for final distribution, you may want to resolve such page-numbering discrepancies to avoid confusing your users. For more information, see page 34 of the *Electronic Publishing Guide,* located on the Acrobat Classroom in a Book CD-ROM.

Editing text

You use the touch-up tool to make small, last-minute corrections to text in a PDF document. This version of *Aesop's Fables* contains one faulty moral, which you will rectify using the touch-up tool.

Correcting a typo

1 Click the Page Only button (▤) to close the overview window.

2 Go to page 7, and read the fable that appears.

Notice that the moral to this tale makes little sense in the context of the story because of the typo in the second line. The correct moral should read: "Beware lest you lose the substance by grasping at the shadow."

3 Click the touch-up tool (**T**) in the toolbar, and move the pointer into the document window. Notice that the pointer changes to an I-beam.

4 Move the I-beam pointer over the second line of the moral, and click between the "g" and "a" in "gasping."

A blinking cursor appears at the point of insertion.

> ...ind to have that also. So he made a snap
> in the water, but as he opened his mouth
> meat fell out, dropped into the water, and
> ...en again.
>
> *Beware lest you lose the substance*
> *by gasping at the shadow.*

5 Type **r** to change the faulty word to "grasping."

6 Click in the blank area of the page to deselect the line of the moral.

Changing the appearance of text

Once you've selected some text using the touch-up tool, you can change the text attributes, such as the spacing, point size, and color.

Note: *You may not have the full array of editing options when editing text in a font that has been embedded. For more information, see "Editing text" in the* Exchange Online Guide.

You should be viewing "The Dog and the Shadow." The entire line of the moral is currently set at black. You'll change the appearance of the word "shadow" to give the moral an accent.

1 Click the touch-up tool, and double-click the word "shadow" to highlight it.

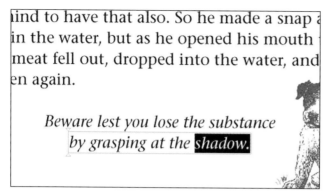

> ind to have that also. So he made a snap
> in the water, but as he opened his mouth
> meat fell out, dropped into the water, and
> en again.
>
> *Beware lest you lose the substance*
> *by grasping at the* shadow.

2 Choose Edit > Text Attributes.

The text attributes window appears. This window contains a variety of controls for setting the properties of the selected text.

3 Make sure that the Font tab is selected, and click the center color selection box.

Macintosh dialog box

A color selection dialog box appears.

4 Choose a new color for the selected text, according to your platform:

• In Windows, click a color swatch, and click OK.

• On the Macintosh, drag the sliders, click in the color wheel, or enter values to change the color. Then press Return.

5 In the text attributes window, enter **20** for the point size.

Windows dialog box

6 Click in the blank area of the document to deselect the word and see the color change.

7 Close the text attributes window.

Although you can use the touch-up tool to edit text, you can only do so one line at a time. As a result, editing large sections of text in Exchange can be a slow and laborious task. In general, you should reserve use of the touch-up tool for minor text edits in PDF.

If you need to change a substantial amount of text in your PDF document, it's best to modify the corresponding pages in your original source file and reconvert them to PDF. You can then replace your old pages with these modified pages.

Using links and bookmarks to play actions

In most cases, you use links and bookmarks to jump to different views of a document. However, you can also use links and bookmarks to execute commands from the menus and to play movies, sound clips, or other actions. For detailed information on the types of actions assignable to links and bookmarks, see the *Exchange Online Guide.*

Creating a link that executes a menu item

1 Go to page 1 of the book and click the Fit Page button(▣).

2 Select the hand tool and move the hand over the button labelled "Full Screen" at the bottom right corner of the page.

Notice that the button is not currently linked. You'll create a link so that users can click the button to display the book in Full Screen mode.

Full Screen mode maximizes the monitor space for page display by hiding the window controls, menu bar, and toolbar.

3 Click the link tool and drag a marquee around the Full Screen button.

4 Under Appearance, for Type, choose Invisible Rectangle; for Highlight, choose Invert. Under Action, for Type, choose Execute Menu Item.

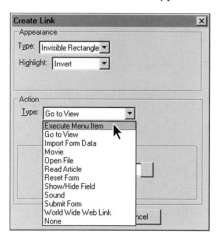

5 Click Edit Menu Item. In the Menu Item Selection window that appears, choose View > Full Screen, and click OK.

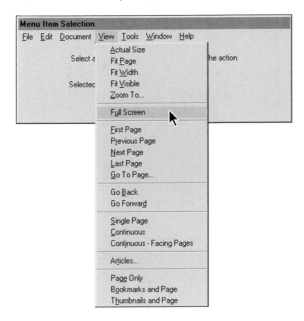

Notice that the command name and a description of its action now appears in the Create Link dialog box.

6 Click Set Link.

7 Click the hand tool and test the link you've created.

In Full Screen mode, use Enter (Windows) or Return (Macintosh) to turn pages.

8 Press Esc to exit Full Screen mode.

Creating a bookmark that plays a sound

1 Click the Bookmarks and Page button to view the bookmark list.

2 Click The Lion and the Mouse bookmark text to jump to that fable.

You'll create a bookmark that will play the moral of this story aloud.

3 Click the page icon for The Lion and the Mouse bookmark to select it.

4 Choose Document > New Bookmark, and name the new bookmark **Mouse Moral**.

5 Drag the page icon for the Mouse Moral bookmark up and to the right until the black insertion bar appears under the "T" in The Lion and the Mouse bookmark.

6 Release the mouse to create a nested bookmark.

7 Click the page icon for this new bookmark, and choose Edit > Properties.

8 For Type, choose Sound. Then click Select Sound.

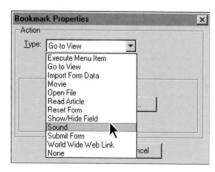

9 Select Mouse.wav (Windows) or Mouse.aif (Macintosh) from the Lesson06 folder, and click Open.

This sound file has been created using a sound-editing program and saved in a format recognizable to Exchange.

10 Click Set Action.

11 Click in the blank area of the overview windows to deselect all bookmarks.

12 Use the hand tool to test your new bookmark.

You will hear the moral if you have the proper audio hardware installed on your system. For more information on sound system requirements and the types of sound file formats you can use with Exchange, see the *Exchange Online Guide.*

13 Choose File > Save As, and save 06work.pdf in your PROJECTS folder.

14 Choose File > Close to close the fables book.

Review

In this lesson, you've practiced making editing changes to the pages in a PDF document. You've learned how to use thumbnails to reorder pages and created a bookmark that plays a sound. Later in this book you'll learn how to add more multimedia features to your PDF documents.

To test your knowledge of the concepts and techniques you learned in this lesson, answer the following questions:

• How can you automate the creation of links and bookmarks?

• How do you change the order of pages in a document?

• What kinds of text attributes can you change from within Exchange?

• How do you select multiple thumbnails?

• How do you insert an entire PDF file into another PDF file?

• How do you insert one page or a range of pages from one PDF file into another?

• What types of actions can you assign to links and bookmarks?

A

Project

Creating an Online Version of a Book

This project guides you through the process of converting a printed book to online format. You'll create a PDF document from the electronic files for the original book layout, and add a variety of hyperlink features to enhance your electronic publication. In the course of this project, you'll review many of the concepts and techniques that were introduced in previous lessons.

In this project, you'll review and learn how to do the following:

• Specify Distiller job options.

• Distill a Postscript file to PDF.

• Create custom bookmarks.

• Create an article thread.

• Replace a page of a PDF file.

• Compare the design differences between different online publications.

This project will take about 35 minutes to complete.

About this project

In this project, you'll work with an abridged version of the *Adobe Illustrator® User Guide,* a printed book written, designed, and produced by Adobe Systems to accompany its desktop illustration program. You'll create an electronic print-on-demand version of the user guide without altering the content or design of the original book. Then you'll compare your print-on-demand guide with another electronic version of the user guide, which has been redesigned and optimized for online viewing.

First, you'll distill the original book file to PDF. For your convenience, we've already created a PostScript version of the original FrameMaker file used to create the user guide.

Setting Distiller options

By now, you've used Acrobat Distiller at least once to convert PostScript files to PDF. But you haven't yet changed any of the job options that control how Distiller converts the file. In most cases, the default Distiller options produce satisfactory results. If you don't get the results you want, you may consider changing some of the options. You can find complete information on job options in the *Distiller Online Guide.*

Before distilling the book file, you'll specify options for file compression and font embedding.

Specifying compression and downsampling settings

Distiller uses a variety of methods that compress the text, line art, and bitmap images in a document to reduce file size. Since smaller files open and display more quickly, the ideal compression setting is one that compresses the file as much as possible without noticeably degrading its quality.

In addition to choosing a compression method, you can downsample bitmap images in your file to reduce the file size. A bitmap image consists of digital units called *pixels,* whose total number determines the file size. When you *downsample* a bitmap image, the information represented by several pixels in the image is combined to make a single larger pixel.

1 Start Acrobat Distiller.

2 Choose Distiller > Job Options.

The Options dialog box lets you control different aspects of the distilling process. These settings appear under different category tabs in the dialog box.

3 Click the General tab, and click Defaults to return the settings to their default positions.

You can click Defaults at any time to reset the job option settings.

4 For Compatibility, choose Acrobat 3.0.

The Acrobat 3.0 compatibility optimizes the distilled file to take full advantage of the new features in Acrobat 3.0.

5 Click the Compression tab.

The Compression options let you specify different compression methods for the color, grayscale, and black-and-white images in your file, and control how much these images are downsampled.

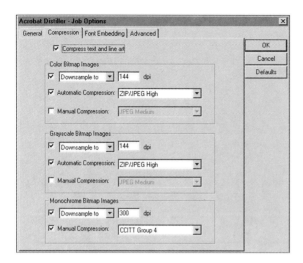

6 Under Color Bitmap Images, in the number field to the right of Downsample To, enter **144**. For Automatic Compression, choose ZIP/JPEG High to use the maximum compression setting.

7 Under Grayscale Bitmap Images, in the number field to the right of Downsample To, enter **144**. For Automatic Compression, choose ZIP/JPEG High.

Downsampling to 144 dpi instead of the default 72 dpi preserves more of the pixel information, and therefore visual detail, of the images in the user guide. These 144-dpi images will also appear sharper and more detailed if they are printed out on a desktop printer.

Embedding fonts

Acrobat's sophisticated font substitution scheme preserves the appearance of standard fonts when your document is converted to PDF. However, if your source document contains display fonts (such as a script font), you need to embed these fonts in the document. Embedding a font includes all the needed font information within the PDF file and ensures that the actual font will display on any system, regardless of whether the fonts are installed on that system.

1 With the Job Options dialog box still open, click the Font Embedding tab.

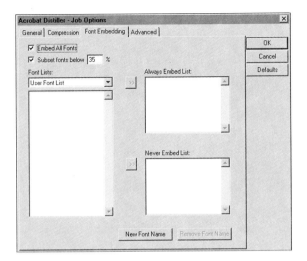

The Font options let you choose which fonts in the document to embed. In this lesson, you'll embed all the fonts that occur in the user guide file.

2 Select Embed All Fonts.

The Subset Fonts option lets you embed only those characters of a font that appear in the document, thus reducing file size. For example, suppose you are embedding a Roman font, which consists of 256 characters, and have a subset setting of 35%. This means that if you use less than 35%, or 90, of the font characters, only those characters are embedded; if you use more than 90 characters, the entire font is embedded.

3 Leave the Subset Fonts option selected and click OK.

Creating the PDF file

1 From Distiller, choose File > Open. Select Ai6ug.ps, located in the Projecta folder, and click Open.

2 Name the file Projecta.pdf, and save it in your PROJECTS folder.

Distiller converts the PostScript file to PDF.

3 Exit or quit Acrobat Distiller.

Viewing the distilled PDF file

Now you'll open the user guide that you just distilled. We've also provided a pre-distilled PDF file for you, in case your distilling process was unsuccessful.

1 Start Acrobat Exchange.

2 Choose File > Open, and do one of the following:

• If you successfully distilled the PostScript file in the previous section, select Projecta.pdf, located in the PROJECTS folder, and click Open.

• If you were not able to distill the PostScript file, select Ai6ug.pdf, located in the Projecta folder, and click Open.

The distilled PDF file contains two user guide chapters, a table of contents, and an index, just as in the original FrameMaker file. The table of contents entries, cross-references, index entries, and text flows in the FrameMaker file have been converted to bookmarks, links, and articles in the PDF file.

You can automatically generate PDF links from files that have been properly formatted in an application that supports this automation capability, such as Adobe FrameMaker or Adobe PageMaker.

3 Click the Bookmarks and Page button (⊞) to display the overview window. If needed, resize the overview window to view the complete bookmark text.

4 Select the hand tool, and click the Contents bookmark to view the table of contents. If needed, adjust the view magnification to display the entire page on your screen.

5 Move the pointer over the contents list and notice that the pointing finger appears over each linked entry.

6 Click the text of a contents entry to jump to its corresponding section of information. Then move your pointer over a column of text and notice the downward pointing arrow inside the hand pointer that indicates an article thread.

7 Click once to enter the article. Press Enter (Windows) or Return (Macintosh) several times to follow the article thread.

8 Click the Index bookmark to view the index listings. Each page number listing links to the appropriate reference in the text.

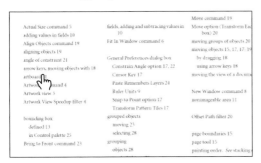

9 Position your pointer over the number next to the "artboard" entry so that the pointing finger appears. Click to jump to the section about the Illustrator artboard.

10 Choose File > Save As, name the file Projecta.pdf, and save it in your PROJECTS folder. You can replace the existing Projecta.pdf file.

The index for this user guide was originally created in Adobe FrameMaker and then converted automatically to a linked PDF index during the distilling process. The following chart outlines the procedure for generating a PDF index from a FrameMaker file.

INDEX CREATION FROM A FRAMEMAKER BOOK FILE You can convert an index generated in FrameMaker to an interactive PDF index whose entries link to the referenced document pages.

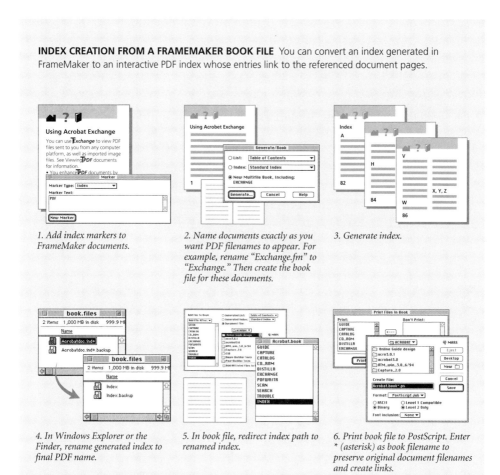

1. Add index markers to FrameMaker documents.

2. Name documents exactly as you want PDF filenames to appear. For example, rename "Exchange.fm" to "Exchange." Then create the book file for these documents.

3. Generate index.

4. In Windows Explorer or the Finder, rename generated index to final PDF name.

5. In book file, redirect index path to renamed index.

6. Print book file to PostScript. Enter * (asterisk) as book filename to preserve original document filenames and create links.

Adding bookmarks

Although the basic bookmarks and links for the book have already been generated, you can still add your own custom bookmarks and links using the tools in Exchange. In this part of the lesson, you'll add some new bookmarks that link just to the charts, or sidebars, in the book.

Creating bookmarks

You'll create three new bookmarks under the Index bookmark.

1 Click the page icon for the Index bookmark. Any bookmarks you create will appear below this selected bookmark.

2 Choose Document > New Bookmark, and name the untitled bookmark **Sidebars.**

You'll create the remaining two bookmarks using the keyboard shortcut for the New Bookmarks command. Many Exchange commands can be executed using keyboard shortcuts, which appear next to the command names in the menus.

3 Press Ctrl+B (Windows) or Command +B (Macintosh) to create a new bookmark, and name it **Work area**.

4 Press Ctrl+B (Windows) or Command +B (Macintosh), and name the new bookmark **Control palette.**

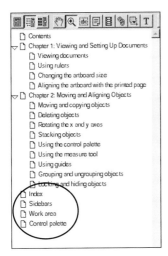

Now you'll nest the Work area and Control palette bookmarks under the Sidebars bookmark.

5 Hold down Shift and click the page icons for the Work area and Control palette bookmarks to select them both, and then release Shift.

6 Click one of the page icons for the selected bookmarks, and drag the bookmarks up and to the right. When the black bar appears under the "S" in the Sidebars bookmark, release the mouse.

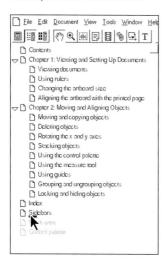

7 Click in the blank area of the overview window to deselect the bookmarks.

Resetting bookmark destinations

Remember from Lesson 5 that bookmark destinations default to the current document view displayed on your screen. Now you'll assign a correct destination or action to each of the new bookmarks you've created.

1 Go to page 11, where the sidebar titled "About the Work Area" appears.

2 If needed, click the Fit Page button to display the whole page. Then use the zoom tool to magnify the sidebar.

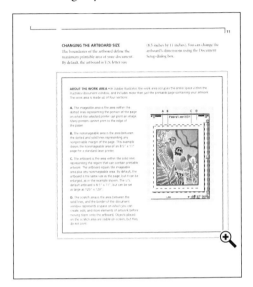

3 Select the hand tool, click the page icon for the Work area bookmark, and choose Document > Reset Bookmark Destination. Click Yes to the confirmation message that appears.

4 Now go to page 25 and click Fit Page. Click the zoom tool and marquee-drag around the sidebar titled "Using the Control palette."

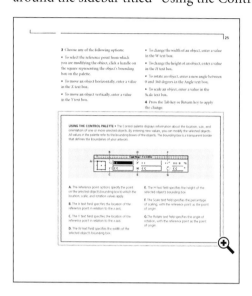

5 Click the hand tool and click the page icon for the Control palette bookmark. Then press Ctrl+R (Windows) or Command+R (Macintosh) to reset the destination of the selected bookmark to the current view, and click Yes to the message that appears.

Next, you'll make the Sidebars bookmark into a placeholder heading for its sub-bookmarks.

6 Click the triangle to the left of the Sidebars bookmark to hide its nested sub-bookmarks.

7 Click the page icon for the Sidebars bookmark to select the bookmark.

8 Choose Edit > Properties, choose None as the action type, and click Set Action (Windows) or OK (Macintosh).

9 Click in the blank area of the overview window to deselect all bookmarks, and click the triangle next to the Sidebars bookmark to display its nested sub-bookmarks.

10 Use the hand tool to test your new bookmarks. Notice that nothing happens when you click the Sidebars bookmark; this bookmark functions not as a link but as a hierarchical placeholder.

11 Click the Page Only button (▣) to close the overview window.

Creating an article thread

At the beginning of this lesson you followed an automatically generated article thread to follow text that spanned a number of nonconsecutive columns and pages. Now you'll use the article tool to create your own thread connecting the short tip segments that appear throughout the user guide.

Defining the article

1 Go to page 5, and click the Fit Page button (▢) to view the entire page.

2 Click the zoom tool (🔍), and marquee-zoom to magnify the top left corner of the page, where a tip appears.

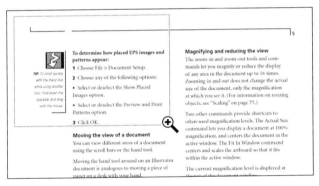

3 Choose Tools > Article to select the article tool. When you first use the article tool, it appears as a crosshair pointer in the document window.

4 Drag a marquee around the tip text.

An article box appears around the enclosed tip, and the pointer changes to the article pointer (⬚).

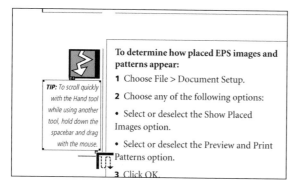

The "2-1" label at the top of the article box indicates that this is the first section of the second article in the file. Now you'll add another article box to continue the thread.

5 Use the page-number box in the status bar to go to page 8. If needed, use the scroll bars to bring the tip in the left margin of the page into view.

6 Drag an article box around the tip on this page. You point with the top left corner of the article pointer.

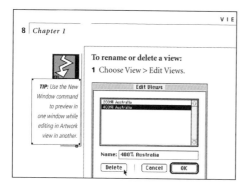

7 Use the page-number box in the status bar to go to page 27, and create an article box around the tip that occurs on that page.

8 Click End Article in the status bar to end the article thread.

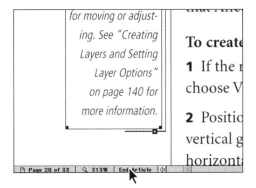

The display returns to the first article box you created, and the Article Properties dialog box appears.

9 Do the following:

• For Title, enter **Tips**, and press Tab.

• For Subject, enter **Shortcuts and suggestions,** and press Tab.

• Leave the Author and Keywords fields blank, and click OK.

Reading the article

1 Click the hand tool, and choose View > Articles to display the list of available articles.

2 Select Tips, and click View.

The contents of the first article box you created appear on-screen. You can control the magnification of article boxes by adjusting the Max "Fit Visible" Magnification preference, set in the General Preferences dialog box.

3 Click the Fit Page button to exit the article.

4 Choose File > Preferences > General to open the General Preferences dialog box.

5 For Max "Fit Visible" Magnification, choose 150, and click OK.

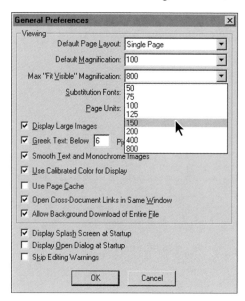

6 Move the hand pointer over the tip on the top left corner of the page, and click to enter the article.

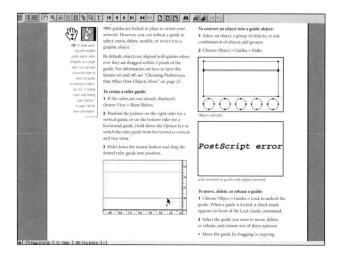

Look at the status bar and notice that the article box now appears at 150% magnification.

7 Use the following techniques to move through the article:

• To advance to the next article section, press Enter (Windows) or Return (Macintosh).

• To move backwards through the article, hold down Shift and press Enter or Return.

• To move to the beginning of the article, hold down Ctrl (Windows) or Option (Macintosh) and click inside the article.

8 Click the Fit Page button to exit the article.

9 If desired, experiment with different Max "Fit Visible" Magnification settings and notice the resulting effects on your article view.

Inserting an article box

You can edit an existing article thread using the article tool at any time. For example, you can delete an article box by clicking inside the box with the article tool and pressing Delete. In this part of the lesson, you'll insert another tip into the article thread you just created.

1 Navigate to page 5, and click Fit Page.

2 Choose Tools > Article, and click inside the tip to select the article box. Handles appear at the corners of an article box when it is selected.

You'll insert a new article box after box 2-1.

3 Move your pointer over the plus sign at the bottom of box 2-1 so that the article pointer appears, and click.

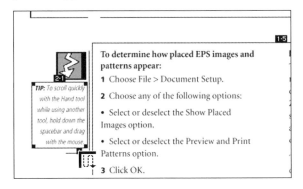

From now on, the pointer appears as the article pointer. In addition, "End Article" appears in the status bar, indicating that you are editing the article thread.

4 Click Next Page to go to page 6. Use the article pointer to drag a box around the tip in the left margin. Notice that this new article box is labelled "2-2."

5 Click End Article in the status bar.

6 Select the hand tool. Choose View > Article, select Tips, and click View to examine your edited article thread.

7 Press Enter (Windows) or Return (Macintosh) to view the new article box you inserted. Click the Fit Page button to exit the article when you have finished viewing it.

Replacing a page

The plain title page that currently opens the document represents the first page that appears in the printed version of the user guide. To make your PDF user guide look more like an actual book, you'll replace this title page with the full-color illustration that was used to create the front cover of the printed guide.

1 Click the First Page button to display the current title page, and click Fit Page.

2 Choose Document > Replace Pages.

3 Select Cover.pdf, located in the Projecta folder, and click Select.

4 In the Replace Pages dialog box, make sure you are replacing page 1, and click OK.

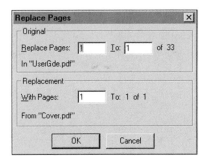

The new cover illustration appears as page 1 of the document.

5 Choose File > Save As, and save Projecta.pdf in your PROJECTS folder. You can replace the existing Projecta.pdf file.

Comparing different online versions of the same book

You may have noticed that you did not revise the content or layout of the user guide in creating the Projecta.pdf document. This print-on-demand document represents the quickest and least expensive option for converting a printed book to online. Now you'll open another PDF version of the user guide that has been redesigned and optimized for online use.

1 Choose File > Open, select Online.pdf, located in the Projecta folder, and click Open. Then choose Window > Tile Vertically to view the two open documents side by side.

2 If needed, adjust the magnification to fit Online.pdf on-screen. The tall and narrow page size has been designed for side-by-side viewing next to the Adobe Illustrator application window; this way, users can conveniently look up reference information without closing their illustration window.

Notice also that Online.pdf contains a hypertext list of elements in the document. A few book elements have been created specially for the optimized online guide.

3 Click How To Use This Guide to jump to the section that explains basic navigational techniques to the user. Click the Go Back button (◀◀) in the toolbar when you have finished viewing the instructions.

4 Click List of Topics to view the text contents of the document.

Notice that you jump to a screen listing the main topic titles.

5 Click Viewing and setting up documents to display the subtopics under this topic.

6 Now click the Projecta.pdf document window to make it active, and go to page 2, the Contents page. Click the Actual Size button (◻) to display this page at 100%.

Compare the table of contents in Projecta.pdf (the print-on-demand guide) with the topic screens in Online.pdf (the optimized online guide). Online.pdf arranges its content listings in nested, hierarchical screens, while Projecta.pdf lists the main topics and their subtopics linearly on the page. Although the linear arrangement follows the conventional organization of a printed book, the hierarchical structure is better suited for an online environment where the most intuitive action involves clicking a link to follow a trail of information.

7 In Projecta.pdf, click Using Rulers under the Chapter 1 heading to jump to that page of text. If needed, use the scroll bars to move the right column of the page into view.

8 Now return to Online.pdf, and click Using Rulers in the list of subtopics. If needed, click Fit Page to view the entire page.

Notice that pages in the optimized online guide have been redesigned so that each topic has its own page. Related topic titles appear as red, linked text.

9 Now click the target icon at the top of the page to return to the parent list of sub-topics, and then click About the Work Area.

This link jumps you to an overview text section that contains its own links to sub-topics and art. Click the Jump to Art icon to view a diagram of the work area with all of its components labelled and linked.

10 Return to Projecta.pdf, and navigate to page 11 to view the linear equivalent of the "About the Work Area" section. If needed, adjust the magnification and use the scroll bar to view the entire section. Compare the text-intensive pages of Projecta.pdf with the more balanced text blocks in Online.pdf.

By breaking longer topics into their subtopic components and placing these sections on separate pages, you minimize the amount of text shown on each page. As a result, you can display text in a larger, clearer typeface that users can read more easily. In addition, the smaller, self-contained pages reduce the need for scrolling and readjusting the page view. Ideally, a user of Online.pdf should be able to navigate to any part of the document solely by clicking linked text and icons in the page.

11 Return to Online.pdf, and click the book icon at the top of the page to return to the opening contents screen. Then click Index.

Like the index for the print-on-demand guide, the page-number listings in the online index link to their referenced section. However, the online index also includes an alphabet tab along the left of the page, which lets you jump to specific parts of the index quickly.

12 Close the Online.pdf and Projecta.pdf files.

Review

In this project, you've reviewed some document editing skills and learned how to create and modify article threads. You've also learned how to execute some commonly used commands by using keyboard shortcuts.

To test your knowledge of the concepts and techniques you learned in this project, answer the following questions:

• How do you generate a PDF index automatically when distilling a FrameMaker file?

• What does Distiller's compression scheme do?

• What are the advantages of embedding fonts?

• How can the table of contents for a printed publication differ from the table of contents for a strictly online publication?

• How do you insert a new article box into an existing article thread?

• How do you end an article thread?

7

Lesson 7

Adding Page Actions, Movies, and Sound to PDF Files

By adding movie and sound clips, you can transform your PDF document into a multimedia experience. Movie and sound files can be integrated into PDF documents as playable clips and as link or bookmark actions.

In this lesson, you'll learn how to do the following:

- Assign a page action.
- Add a movie to a document and set the movie's appearance and playback properties.
- Edit the playback properties of an added movie clip.
- Add a link that plays a movie clip.
- Add a link that plays a sound clip.

This lesson will take about 30 minutes to complete.

Using movie and sound files

You can use media clips with your PDF documents in a variety of ways. The movie tool in Exchange lets you add movies and sounds as playable clips in your document. You can also assign movies and sounds as actions that automatically play when you click a link, bookmark, or button, or when you open or close a page.

When you add a media clip to a PDF document using the movie tool, or when you add a movie clip as an action, the clip does not become part of the document; the document simply contains a pointer that references the media file. If you plan to distribute your PDF document, you must also include these sound or movie files along with the document. However, when you add a sound clip as an action, the sound clip does become part of the PDF file; in this case, you do not have to include the original sound file.

Although you can add movie and sound clips to a PDF document, you cannot create or edit the content of these files using any of the Acrobat programs. You must create your clip using a sound- or video-editing program first, and then save the file in a format that Acrobat can recognize. For a list of suitable sound and movie formats, see the *Exchange Online Guide*.

Opening the work file

1 Start Acrobat Exchange.

2 Choose File > Open.

3 Select Geology.pdf, located in the Lesson07 folder, and click Open.

The Field Guide is designed to provide park visitors with an interactive, multimedia tour of Mount Rainier's services, sights, geology, and history. Visitors can use links to follow their own path of interest through the document and to view successively more detailed information about a desired topic.

Using page actions

You can add sounds and movies as *page actions* to a PDF document. Page actions occur when a page is opened or closed. First, you will open a page that has an action assigned to it; then you will assign your own page action.

Activating a page action

Click About the Park and listen.

A sound plays when the "About the Park" page opens. This is an example of a page action. (You will hear a sound if you have the proper hardware components installed.)

Assigning a page action

Now, you will assign a page action to the history contents page. You should be viewing page 2 of the Field Guide.

1 Click History.

2 Choose Document > Set Page Action.

3 Select Page Open from the When this happens box, and click Add.

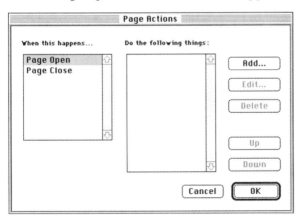

4 In the Add an Action dialog box, for Type, choose Sound; then click Select Sound.

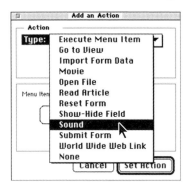

5 Select the Sound2.wav (Windows) or Sound2.aif (Macintosh) file in the Lesson07 folder, and click Open.

6 Click Set Action, and then click OK.

You have just assigned a sound to play whenever this page is opened. Now you'll try it out.

7 Click the Next Page button.

8 Click the Go Back button and listen for the sound.

9 Click the First Page button.

10 Click the page-number box in the status bar, enter **3**, and click OK.

The sound plays again when you open the history page. From now on, you will hear the sound whenever you open the page, regardless of the method you use to open it.

Actions can also be assigned to occur when a page closes. And you can assign more than one action to occur and control the order in which they occur. For more information, see "Adding more buttons with multiple actions" on page 222.

Using movies in PDF files

You activate a movie in a PDF document much as you activate a link. A certain area on the page is designated as the active area for the movie; clicking in this hot spot plays the movie.

You'll practice activating an existing movie in the Field Guide and also adding a new movie to the document.

Playing a movie

You should be viewing page 3 of the Field Guide.

1 Click Geologic History to find out more about the park's natural formations.

The first geologic history screen appears.

2 If needed, adjust the view magnification to display the entire page on-screen.

Notice that the topic window contains page navigation features for moving to the next screen. The Geologic History series spans six screens.

Notice that the page number on the page reads "1 of 6," while the page number in the status bar reads "4 of 11." When you create a custom page-numbering sequence in a document, you can expect this sequence to differ from the page numbering shown in the status bar, which always regards the first page of a document as page 1. For more information on working around such page numbering conflicts, see the *Electronic Publishing Guide,* located on the Acrobat Classroom in a Book CD-ROM.

3 Click the forward arrow at the bottom right corner of the page to go to screen 2 of the sequence (page 5 in the status bar). Then click the About Volcanoes frame to follow its link.

4 Move the pointer over the Volcano Movie graphic. Notice that the pointer changes to a movie frame pointer.

5 Click the Volcano Movie graphic to show the film clip.

The movie plays inside a *floating window* that appears in front of the document temporarily. You can also have a movie play directly in the document page, without a floating window.

6 Click Go Back when you're finished viewing the movie to return to the Geologic History section.

Adding a movie

1 Click the forward arrow in the page to go to the next screen in the Geologic History sequence. Continue clicking the forward arrow until you arrive at screen 5 of the sequence (page 8 in the status bar).

2 Click About Glaciers to view its information screen. You'll add a movie about glaciers to the About Glaciers screen and have it play directly inside its activation area in the document.

3 If needed, click the Actual Page button to return to 100% view.

Because movies have a set number of pixels and therefore a set size, it's important to keep the magnification at 100% to prevent the added movie clip from being scaled inadvertently.

4 Click the movie tool (▦) in the toolbar.

5 Click in the center of the black box to set the location for the movie. Be sure to click, not drag, with the movie tool.

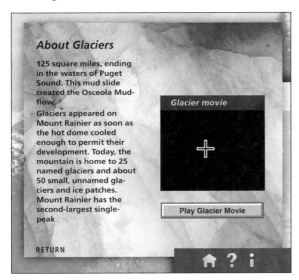

When you click to place a movie, the pixel size of the movie frame determines the activation area for the clip in the document. You can also drag with the movie tool to specify the activation area, but this is not advised, since the movie frame must then be stretched or compressed to fit into the specified area. This resizing often results in distorted image quality.

When you're adding a movie using a floating window, however, you can drag freely with the movie tool to set the activation area. The size of a floating window is determined by its Movie Properties setting, not by the activation area you set by dragging.

6 Select Glacier.mov, located in the Lesson07 folder, and click Open.

The Movie Properties dialog box appears. This dialog box lets you set the appearance and playback behavior of the movie. You can also specify whether to place a poster (a still image of the first movie frame) in the document.

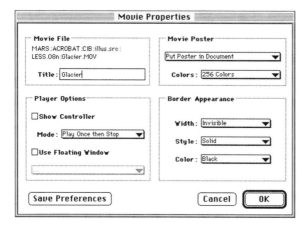

7 For Title, enter **Glacier.** For Movie Poster, choose Put Poster in Document.

8 Under Player Options, select Show Controller. For Mode, choose Repeat Play. If needed, deselect Floating Window (Windows) or Use Floating Window (Macintosh).

Selecting Show Controller displays the controller bar, which lets the viewer stop, pause, and rewind the movie.

9 Under Border Appearance, for Width, select Invisible. Then click OK.

The movie poster appears in the document.

10 Move the pointer over the poster until the four-headed move arrow appears. Drag the movie poster inside the Glacier Movie box.

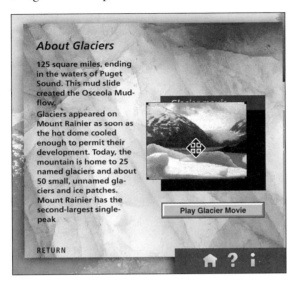

You can also resize the poster by dragging the poster's corners. However, remember that resizing the movie area may result in distorted image quality.

11 Click the hand tool and test the movie you just added. Use the buttons in the controller bar to pause, rewind, and fast forward through the movie.

You can stop a movie at any time by pressing Esc or clicking outside the movie image.

Adding a link that plays a movie

In addition to linking different page views, links can be used to perform actions such as playing movie or sound clips. You must first add a movie to a document before you can create a link that activates it, and the link you create must be on the same page as the movie. In this part of the lesson, you'll create a new link that plays the glacier movie you've already added.

1 Select the link tool (🔗), and drag a marquee around the Play Glacier Movie button.

2 In the Create Link dialog box, under Appearance, for Type, choose Invisible Rectangle. Under Action, for Type, choose Movie.

3 Click Select Movie. For Select Movie, choose Glacier. For Select Operation, choose Play, and click OK.

4 Click Set Link.

5 Use the hand tool to test your new link.

Editing movie properties

You can change the playback properties of a movie at any time.

1 Click the movie tool, and double-click within the glacier image to display the Movie Properties dialog box.

2 Under Player Options, deselect Show Controller. For Mode, choose Play Once Then Stop. Then click OK.

3 Select the hand tool, and click Play Glacier Movie to see the modified playback properties.

Using sounds in a document

You can add sounds and movies to a document using the movie tool. You can also assign movies and sounds as actions that are played when you click a bookmark or link.

Activating an existing sound

1 Click the page-number box in the status bar. Enter **6** and click OK to view the screen containing the About mountains image.

2 Using the hand tool, move the pointer over the About mountains image. Notice that the pointer turns into the movie frame pointer.

The movie frame pointer indicates that either a movie or sound clip can be activated.

3 Click the About Mountains image to play the sound that has been added to this location.

Adding a sound as a link action

Next, you'll create a link that plays a sound as an action.

1 Click the forward arrow on the page to view the screen that contains the About mudflows image.

You'll add a sound that will be activated by clicking the About mudflows image.

2 Click the link tool (🔗) in the toolbar.

3 Drag a marquee that surrounds the About mudflows image.

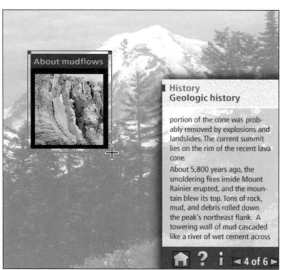

4 Under Appearance, for Type, choose Invisible Rectangle. For Highlight, choose None.

5 Under Action, for Type, choose Sound, and click Select Sound.

6 Do one of the following:

• In Windows, select Mud.wav, located in the Lesson07 folder, and click Open. (If you do not see the file listed, for Files of type, choose All Files.)

• On the Macintosh, select Mud.aif, located in the Lesson07 folder, and click Open.

7 Click Set Link.

8 Click the hand tool, and move the pointer over the About mudflows image. The pointing finger pointer indicates that you are positioned over a link.

9 Click the link to play the sound you just added.

10 Choose File > Save As, name the file 07work.pdf, and save it in your PROJECTS folder.

11 Choose File > Close to close the document.

Review

In this lesson, you learned how to assign page actions to specific pages and how to add movie and sound clips to a PDF document. In the following lessons, you'll learn how you can use interactive buttons and forms to enhance a multimedia PDF document.

To test your knowledge of the concepts and techniques you learned in this lesson, answer the following questions:

• What kinds of actions can you assign as page actions?

• When using the movie tool to add a movie to a document, why should you click instead of drag?

• What is a movie poster?

• Name three ways in which you can add sound to a PDF document.

• Can you edit the content of movie and sound clips from within Exchange?

8

Lesson 8

Adding Buttons

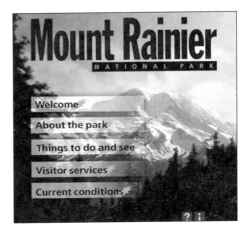

Buttons provide an effective way for you to add creative and stylish interactive features to your PDF documents. Like links, buttons let you jump to different destination views and play actions. In addition, you can customize the appearance of buttons by importing icons.

In this lesson, you will learn how to do the following:

• Activate existing buttons and add your own to a document.

• Duplicate a button across multiple pages.

• Add buttons that show and hide other button fields.

• Add a buttons that links to the World Wide Web.

• Set the opening display of a document.

This lesson will take about 40 minutes to complete.

Using and adding buttons

Like links and bookmarks, buttons can link to a particular destination or play an action. But unlike links and bookmarks, buttons offer the following three additional capabilities:

• Buttons can activate a series of actions, not just a single action.

• A button can have alternate appearances, according to the mouse behavior over the button.

• You can duplicate buttons across a range of pages, thereby simplifying the task of adding repeat buttons to a document.

You use the form tool (📄) to add buttons to a PDF document. In Exchange, buttons are a type of form field. For detailed information on the other types of form fields, see Lesson 9.

Using interactive buttons

In this lesson, you'll work with the camping section of the Mount Rainier Field Guide. This document already contains some buttons that help ease navigation to informational sections such as the index and the "How to use this guide" page. You'll try out these existing buttons, and then add your own.

1 Start Acrobat Exchange.

2 Choose File > Open, select Visit.pdf, located in the Lesson08 folder, and click Open. A visitor's brochure about Mount Rainier opens.

3 Take a moment to page through the document. If needed, click the Fit Page button to view the document pages in their entirety. Notice the gold icons that appear at the bottom of each page.

4 Go to page 3. Click the hand tool, and move your pointer over the ![i] icon at the bottom of page. The hand pointer turns into an arrow, indicating that you are positioned over a button.

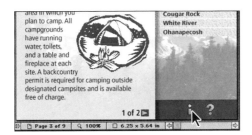

5 Click the ![i] button to jump immediately to the index for this document.

6 Click the Go Back button in the toolbar.

7 Now click the ![?] button at the bottom of the page to link to the "Welcome" page.

These easily recognizable buttons let you jump instantly to their respective informational sections from any page in the document.

Adding buttons

Now you will add a button of your own, and then duplicate it across the relevant pages. You will add a "home" button that brings the user back to page 1 of the Field Guide, the "home" page.

1 Go to page 4 of the document.

2 Click the form tool (🖳) in the toolbar.

The form borders for the two existing buttons appear, enclosing the names of the buttons.

3 Drag to make a box about the same size and to the left of the other buttons at the bottom of the page.

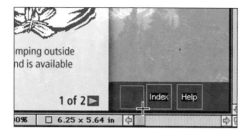

The Field Properties dialog box appears. This dialog box lets you name, format, and optionally assign an action to the new button.

4 For Name, type **Home**, and for Type, choose Button.

5 Click the Button Options tab. For Highlight, choose Push; for Layout, choose Icon only.

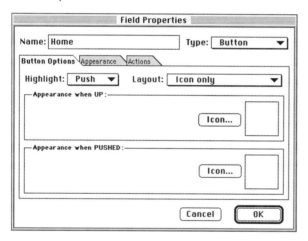

The Highlight option determines the highlight appearance of the button when it is activated, and the Layout option determines the graphical layout of the button. Buttons can display as a line of text, an icon, or a combination of text and icon. You can use text and icons that already exist in the document, or you can import text and icons to represent the buttons. You can only import icons that have been saved in PDF. See the following illustration for examples of the different layout options.

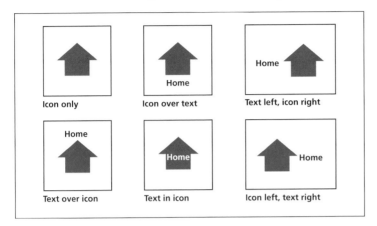

You can specify up to two icons for the same button—one icon to represent the button when the mouse is in the up position over the button, and another to represent the button when the mouse is pushed.

6 Under Appearance when UP, click Icon.

7 Click Browse. Select Home.pdf, located in the Buttons folder inside the Lesson08 folder, and click OK or Open.

The Home.pdf file contains some premade "home" icons for your use. A preview of the first page of the file appears in the Select Appearance dialog box.

8 Click OK to accept the displayed image as the UP icon.

Now you'll use another page from Home.pdf as the button icon when the mouse is pushed.

9 Under Appearance when PUSHED, click Icon.

The Home.pdf preview appears in the Select Appearance dialog box.

10 Click in the scroll bar until you see "2 out of 2" in the preview window, and click OK to accept the displayed icon.

Storing similar button icons as separate pages in a PDF file makes it easy for you to scroll through the previews until you find the icon you want.

When you create a button icon, keep in mind that the icon will automatically shrink to fit the box you create for the button area in the document. You should create button icons at approximately the size you wish to display them in your document.

 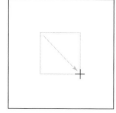 

Original size   *Button field size*   *Size of button*

Note: When creating your icons in your illustration, drawing, or photo-editing program, be sure to place them on a page that is at least 1 inch by 1 inch—the minimum size page allowed as a PDF document. If you want the icon to appear smaller than 1 inch by 1 inch, you will have to allow it to shrink to fit the size of the box you draw with the form tool.

11 Click the Appearance tab. Deselect Border Color and Background Color. For Style, choose Solid.

Now you'll assign the appropriate "home" action to your button.

12 Click the Actions tab.

You specify different actions to occur depending on the behavior of the mouse over the button. The following list describes the various mouse behaviors to which you can assign button actions:

• *Mouse Up* specifies releasing the mouse button.

• *Mouse Down* specifies depressing the mouse button.

• *Mouse Enter* specifies moving the mouse into the button field.

• *Mouse Exit* specifies moving the mouse out of the button field.

We recommend assigning most actions to the Mouse Up behavior. This way, if a user decides that they do not want a particular action to occur, they can simply drag their pointer away from the button field to avoid activating the action.

13 Select Mouse Up, and click Add.

14 For Type, choose Execute Menu Item. Click Edit Menu Item.

15 Choose View > First Page, and click OK, and click Set Action, and then click OK.

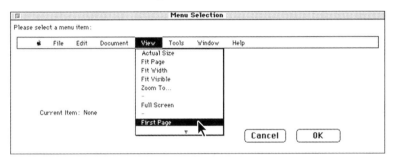

The button is added to your document page.

16 Click the hand tool, move the pointer over your new home button, and hold down the mouse.

Notice that the appearance of the button changes when you depress the mouse.

17 Release the mouse to jump to the first page of the Field Guide.

18 Click Go Back to return to page 4.

If needed, you can easily adjust the size and position of the home button so that it matches the other two buttons on the page.

To resize the home button, click the form tool, click the home button to select it, and drag one of the corner handles. To move the button, position the form tool inside the button and drag.

Duplicating the button

Now that you've created a button that returns the user to the home page, you'll duplicate that button to the other pages in the document. Duplicating a button saves you from the tedious work of recreating the button for each relevant page.

1 Click the form tool (🖳).

2 Click the home button once to select it. Handles appear at the four corners of the button field when a button is selected.

3 Choose Edit > Fields > Duplicate.

4 In the Duplicate Fields dialog box, click From, enter **2** for the start of the page range, and press Tab. Enter **9** for the end of the page range, and click OK. You do not need a home button on the first page.

5 Select the hand tool, and click the Next Page button a few times to see the duplicated home button.

6 Click the home button at the bottom of the current page. You go to the "home" page.

7 Choose File > Save As. Name the file 08work.pdf, and save it in the Lesson08 folder.

Because 08work.pdf contains a link to another document in the Lesson08 folder, you must save it in the Lesson08 folder to preserve the link. PDF documents that are linked to each other must remain in their relative folder locations.

Note: When you duplicate buttons across pages that have been rotated, the buttons may appear in unexpected locations. If this happens, delete the button from the problem pages, and re-add the button manually.

Adding a print button

1 Go to page 4. If needed, adjust the view to display the entire page on-screen.

2 Click the Information Sheet link to open the Camping.pdf document.

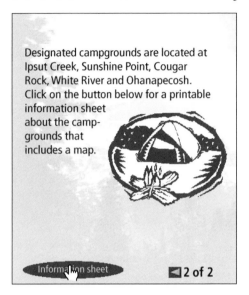

Notice that the camping page plays a sound clip as an open page action.

This page contains important information about the campgrounds in the park. You'll add a button that opens the Print dialog box so that users can print out the page for handy reference.

3 If needed, scroll down to display the bottom of the page, and click the form tool (🖳) in the toolbar.

4 Drag a box as shown in the following illustration.

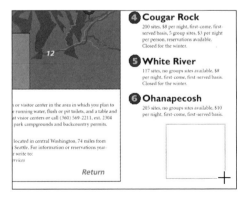

5 For Name, type **Print,** and for type, choose Button.

6 Click the Button Options tab. For Highlight, choose None; for Layout, choose Icon top, text bottom.

7 Under Appearance when UP, for Text, enter **Print this page,** and click Icon.

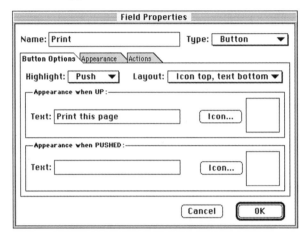

8 Click Browse. Select Printer.pdf, located in the Buttons folder inside the Lesson08 folder, and click OK or Open.

9 Click OK to accept the previewed icon.

Buttons do not have to have alternate appearances. In this case, you will give this button only one appearance, and ignore the Appearance when PUSHED option.

10 Click the Appearance tab. If needed, deselect Border Color and Background Color. For Style, choose Solid.

11 For Font, choose Helvetica Bold, and set the color to black and the point size to 12. Select the Don't Print option to keep the button from appearing on a printout.

12 Click the Actions tab. Select Mouse Up, and click Add.

13 For Type, choose Execute Menu Item, and click Edit Menu Item.

14 In the Menu Item Selection window, choose File > Print, and click OK. Click Set Action, and then click OK. The button is added to the page.

15 Select the hand tool and click your new button.

Note: If the text is cut off, you will need to resize the button field. Select the form tool, click the field, and drag one of the handles to resize the field. Select the hand tool to view the results.

16 The Print dialog box appears. If you would like to print this page, click Print. If not, click Cancel.

Buttons can execute any menu item in the Exchange or Reader menus. But keep in mind that Acrobat Reader users do not have access to all of the menu items available in Acrobat Exchange. If you are not sure if a button will execute a menu item when activated in Reader, try it out.

Editing a button

You can easily change the appearance or action of an existing button.

1 Click the form tool (🖹), and double-click the Print button to open the Field Properties dialog box.

2 Click the Button Options tab. For Layout, choose Text top, icon bottom, and click OK.

3 Select the hand tool. As you can see, the button layout has changed.

4 Continue to experiment with the button layout by double-clicking the button field with the form tool, or go on to the next section.

Using the Show-Hide Field action

Buttons, links, bookmarks, and page actions can be used to show or hide a form field. Since form fields can include a combination of text and graphics, you can alternate showing and hiding a form field to create an interesting visual effect. In this section, you will see how the Show-Hide Field action works and then set up a field to show-hide another field.

We have already set up a field to show and hide another field in the campground page. The hidden field is shown when your pointer enters the other field's border. The field is hidden again when your pointer exits the other field's border.

1 Click the Fit Page button (▢) in the toolbar, then click the Fit Width button (▣).

2 Select the hand tool, and move your pointer over the ❶ icon in the map. As you do, an illustration of the Ipsut Creek Campground is displayed in the upper right corner of the page.

Before

After

3 Move your pointer away from the ❶ icon. The Ipsut Creek Campground illustration is hidden again.

Assigning the Show-Hide Field action

To create the effect just shown for another campground, you will add two new form fields.

1 Click the form tool (▤). The existing form fields appear in the page.

First you'll create the field that will be shown and hidden.

2 Drag to draw a box in the upper right corner of the page that just encloses the existing Ipsut Creek Map button field.

3 For Name, enter **Mowich Lake Map**, and for Type, choose Button.

4 Click the Button Options tab. For Highlight, choose Push, and for Layout, choose Icon only.

5 Under Appearance when UP, click Icon.

6 Click Browse. Select Mowich.pdf, located in the Lesson08 folder, and click OK or Open.

7 Click OK to accept the previewed image as the button.

8 Click the Appearance tab. If needed, deselect Border Color and Background Color, and for Style, choose Solid. Then click OK.

Now you'll create the button on the campgrounds map that will activate the Show-Hide Field action.

9 Drag a box around the ❷ icon on the campgrounds map.

10 For Name, enter 2, and for Type, choose Button.

You will not assign an icon or appearance to this button. Instead, you'll assign actions to occur when the mouse enters and exits the field border.

11 Click the Actions tab. Select Mouse Enter, and click Add.

12 For Type, choose Show-Hide Field, and click Edit.

13 Select Mowich Lake Map, click Show, and click OK. Then click Set Action.

14 Select Mouse Exit, and click Add.

15 For Type, choose Show-Hide Field, and click Edit.

16 Select Mowich Lake Map, click Hide, and click OK. Then click Set Action.

17 Click OK to close the Field Properties dialog box.

18 Select the hand tool, and pass the pointer back and forth over the **2** icon in the campgrounds map. (You may have to pass the hand over the icon to hide the map in the beginning.)

Notice that the Mowich Lake map appears and disappears as the mouse enters and exits the field's border.

Adding a text-only button that links to the World Wide Web

As you've seen, buttons do not have to have icons—they can have no appearance or consist of only a text display. In this part of the lesson, you will add a text-only button that links to the World Wide Web.

1 Scroll down to view the bottom part of the campgrounds page.

2 Select the form tool (🖳).

3 Drag to draw a rectangular box along the bottom edge of the page, as shown in the following illustration.

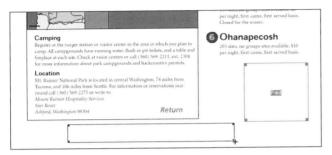

4 For Name, enter **URL**, and for Type, choose Button.

5 Click the Button Options tab. For Highlight, choose None, and for Layout, choose Text only.

6 Under Appearance when UP, for Text, enter **Mount Rainier Web Site**.

You'll give this button a beveled, gray appearance.

7 Click the Appearance Tab. Select Border Color and Background Color. The Border Color and Background Color should be gray; if needed, click the appropriate color box to access the system palette and set the color to gray.

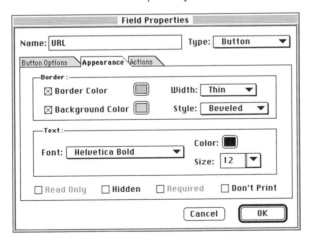

8 For Width, choose Medium, and for Style, choose Beveled.

9 For Font, choose Helvetica Bold, and set the point size to 12. Click the color box to access the system palette, choose a color other than gray, and click OK (Windows) or press Return (Macintosh). Select Don't Print to prevent the button from printing out.

10 Click the Actions tab. Select Mouse Up, and click Add.

11 For Type, choose World Wide Web Link, and click Edit URL.

12 Enter **http://www.adobe.com**, and click OK. Click Set Action, and then click OK. (For the sake of this lesson, you will link to Adobe's Web site.)

13 Select the hand tool and click your new button. If you have a connection to the Internet, you can connect to the Adobe Web site.

14 Choose File > Save As, name the file Camping2.pdf, and save it in the Lesson08 folder.

15 Choose File > Close to close the campgrounds page.

Determining the opening display of a document

In some cases, you may want to control how a particular document displays when it is opened. For example, you may want the document to open in Full Screen mode or to a specific page other than the first page. You can set these preferences easily using the Open Info dialog box.

1 If 08work.pdf is not already open, choose File > Open, select 08work.pdf in the Lesson08 folder, and click Open.

2 Choose File > Document Info > Open.

The Open Info dialog box contains a number of display options for the opened document. For a description of all these options, see the *Exchange Online Guide.*

3 Select Open in Full Screen Mode, and click OK.

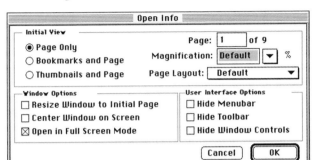

4 Choose File > Save As. Name the file 08work2.pdf and save it in the Lesson08 folder.

5 Choose File > Close.

6 Choose File > Open, and reopen 08work2.pdf from the Lesson08 folder.

Notice how the document opens in Full Screen mode, hiding the menu, tool, and status bars.

7 Press Enter (Windows) or Return (Macintosh) to progress through the document.

You can use Full Screen mode for online presentations or just to enhance the display of a document on-screen.

8 Press Esc to exit Full Screen mode.

9 Choose File > Close to close the file.

Review

In this lesson, you learned how to add navigational aids, execute menu items, and show and hide fields using buttons. Buttons add a new dimension to the level of interactivity that you can use in your PDF documents. As you experiment further with buttons, you will find new ways to use them to enhance your documents.

To test your knowledge of the concepts and techniques you learned in this lesson, answer the following questions:

• What file format must a graphic be saved in before you can use it as a button icon?

- If your original button icon is 5 inches by 5 inches in your graphics program and the field you draw in a PDF file is 3 inches by 3 inches, what size will the button icon appear in the PDF file?

- What is a mouse behavior?

- How can you make a button quit Exchange or Reader?

- Can a link or bookmark show or hide a field?

- Which style gives the appearance of a button without using an icon?

9

Lesson 9
Creating Forms

Acrobat Exchange allows you to create form fields that can be filled out by a user in Acrobat Reader or Exchange. If all the proper software and hardware components are in place, form data can be submitted over the Web and collected in a database just like HTML forms. In this lesson, you will fill out form fields, create form fields, and learn about submitting forms over the World Wide Web.

In this lesson, you will learn how to do the following:

• Fill out a form in a PDF document.

• Export form data.

• Import form data.

• Add form fields, and format those fields.

• Understand how to submit forms over the Web.

This lesson will take about 30 minutes to complete.

Working with forms online

With Acrobat, it's easy to convert your existing paper and electronic forms to PDF, and then use Exchange to create PDF form fields. Using an existing form lets you maintain your organization's corporate identity and branding, and saves you from having to recreate the form design itself.

Many forms require the same information—name, address, phone number, and so on. Wouldn't it be nice if you could enter that data once and use it again and again with the various forms that you have to fill out? Acrobat's ability to import and export form data makes it possible for you to populate different forms with the same set of data.

In this part of the lesson, you will fill out a personal information form, export the data, and then import the data into another form.

Filling out a form

1 Start Acrobat Exchange.

2 Choose File > Open, select Form1.pdf, located in the Lesson09 folder, and click Open.

This electronic form was designed using a page layout application and then distilled to PDF. Form fields have been created so that you can fill out the form from within Exchange.

3 Select the hand tool.

4 Move the pointer just to the right of the "Name" line. When the pointer changes to an I-beam, click to set an insertion point, type your name, and press Tab.

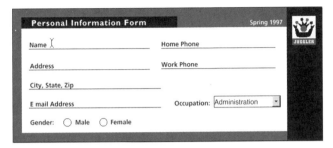

5 Fill out all the text fields, pressing Tab to progress through the fields.

6 For Gender, click the appropriate radio button.

7 To view the list of occupational titles, position your pointer over the down arrow in the Occupation field, and click (Windows) or hold down the mouse (Macintosh). Highlight an item in the pop-up list to select it.

Now that you've filled out your personal information, you'll export the data to a file that contains just your personal information.

8 Choose File > Export > Form Data. Name the file Pif.fdf (Pif for personal information form) and save it in your PROJECTS folder (.fdf is the extension commonly assigned to form data files).

9 Choose File > Close. You don't need to save the changes because the data you entered has already been saved in the exported Pif.fdf file.

Importing data

Now, you will open another form and import the Pif.fdf file to populate the common fields with the personal data you just entered.

1 Choose File > Open, select Form2.pdf, located in the Lesson09 folder, and click Open.

2 Choose File > Import > Form Data. Select Pif.fdf, located in the PROJECTS folder, and click Select (Windows) or Open (Macintosh). The personal information fields are automatically populated.

3 Make sure the hand tool is selected, and fill out the remaining fields. If needed, scroll down to display the bottom of the form.

4 Choose File > Save As. Name the file Forma.pdf, and save it in your PROJECTS folder.

5 To clear all the form fields, click the Reset button at the bottom of the page. You will learn how to set up a reset button later in this lesson.

6 Choose File > Close. Do not save the file.

You can import a form data file repeatedly to fill in multiple forms as long as those forms use the same naming scheme as the original form from which you exported your data. A worldwide standard for naming seems unlikely, but it is certainly possible to create a standard within an organization. You can consistently name fields that ask for the same information with the same name. For example, an address field can always be named *Address* and a home phone field can always be named *Home Phone* (keep in mind that form field names are case sensitive).

In the next section, you will learn how to add a form field, and then name and format it.

Adding form fields

You'll be adding form fields to an electronic order form for Juggler Toys, a fictitious toy manufacturing company. But first, you'll take a look at a completed version of the form that already contains the final form fields.

Examining the completed file

1 Choose File > Open, select Finalfrm.pdf, located in the Lesson09 folder, and click Open.

2 Select the hand tool, and experiment with filling out the different fields to become acquainted with this form.

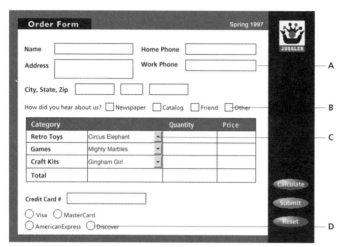

A. Text field *B.* Check box *C.* Combo box *D.* Radio button

Take a moment to notice how the check boxes, pop-up menus, and radio buttons work. Also notice that the Submit button does not submit any data. The Submit button only works from within a Web browser window. To see how a submit button works, use a compatible Web browser such as Netscape Navigator™ 3.0 to navigate to http://www.adobe.com/special/acrobat/demos/forms/finalfrm.pdf. Adobe has set up a fictitious form to give you an idea of how forms work over the Web. Feel free to fill out the form and submit it.

In order for a submit button to work properly over the Web, a Common Gateway Interface (CGI) application must be running on a Web server to collect the submitted data. Usually this CGI application is set up by a Web server administrator. For information contact your Web server administrator or see the Acrobat Web site (http://www.adobe.com/special/acrobat/moreinfo).

3 Choose File > Close to close the final order form. Do not save the file.

Adding text fields

Now you will open the unfinished version of the order form and add the appropriate form fields.

1 Choose File > Open, select Form3.pdf, located in the Lesson09 folder, and click Open.

2 Click the form tool (⬚) in the toolbar. As you can see from the field borders that appear, some of the form fields have already been added for you.

3 Drag to draw a box inside the Name box on the form. The form box should sit inside the existing box so that any text the user enters remains within the box.

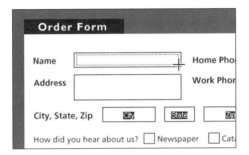

The Field Properties dialog box appears. For a complete description of all the options available in this dialog box, see the *Exchange Online Guide*.

4 For Name, enter **Name**, and for Type, choose Text.

5 Click the Appearance tab.

6 Deselect Border Color and Background Color.

Because the form design has already defined the boundaries of the Name field, you don't need to outline the field with color.

7 Make sure the Text Color is set to black. For Font, choose Helvetica, and set the point size to 10.

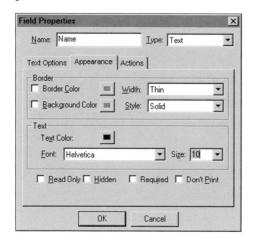

8 Leave the defaults on the Text Options and Actions tabs, and click OK to add the Name text field to the form.

9 Drag to make a box inside the Address box on the form.

10 For Name, enter **Address**, and for Type, choose Text.

11 Click the Text Options tab and select Multi-line.

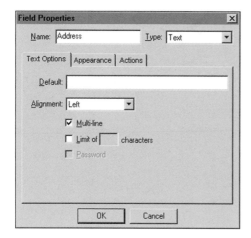

12 Leave the defaults on the Appearance and Actions tabs, and click OK.

The City, State, Zip, and phone fields have already been added to the file for you.

Adding check boxes

Check boxes allow a user to make multiple selections from a group of items. You will add check boxes to this form to allow your users to tell you how they heard about Juggler Toys.

1 Drag to make a box inside the box just to the left of the word "Newspaper" on the form.

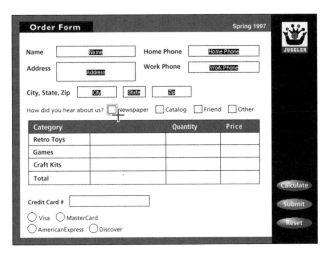

2 For Name, enter **Newspaper**, and for Type, choose Check Box.

3 Click the Check Box Options tab. For Check Style, choose Check.

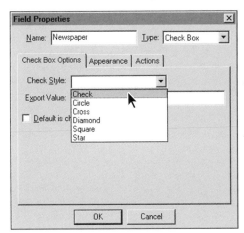

4 Click the Appearance tab.

5 Deselect Border Color and Background Color, and click OK to add the check box to the form.

6 Make three more check box fields inside the boxes next to the Catalog, Friend, and Other options in the form. Name these fields **Catalog**, **Friend**, and **Other**, respectively. Accept the formatting and appearance options that have already been set in the Field Properties dialog box.

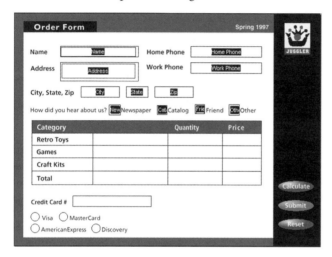

Later in this lesson, you'll learn how to save time by duplicating similar form fields, instead of recreating each field with the form tool.

7 Select the hand tool, and click inside the newly created check box fields. Notice that you can select more than one check box.

Adding a combo box

A *combo box* consists of a list of items that appear in a pop-up menu.

1 Select the form tool, and drag to draw a box inside the cell just to the right of the Retro Toys category on the form.

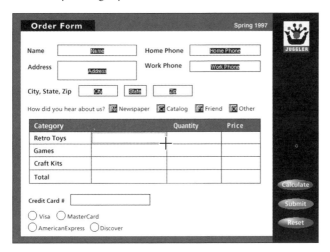

2 For Name, enter **Retro Toys**, and for Type, choose Combo Box.

3 Click the Combo Box Options tab.

Now you will enter the names of the items you wish to appear in the combo box.

4 For Item, enter **Little Red Corvette**, and click Add.

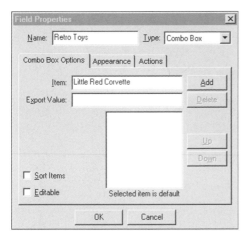

Little Red Corvette is added to the combo box list at the bottom of the dialog box, and the Item field is cleared for you to enter additional items.

5 For Item, enter **57 Chevy**, and click Add.

6 For Item, enter **Circus Elephant**, and click Add.

All three items now appear in the combo box list, in the order in which you added them.

7 Select the Sort Items option to rearrange the items in alphabetical order.

8 Click the Appearance tab.

9 Deselect Border Color and Background Color, and click OK.

10 Select the hand tool, position the pointer over the arrow in the new field, and click (Windows) or hold down the mouse (Macintosh) to view the pop-up list of items.

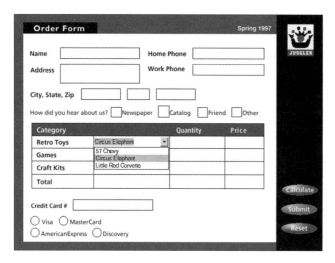

If you like, you can add other combo boxes for the Games and Craft Kits categories. Just follow the procedure outlined in this section, but enter the items shown in the Finalfrm.pdf file.

Adding radio buttons

Unlike check boxes, which let you make multiple selections from a group of items, radio buttons let you select only one item. The important point to remember when creating radio buttons is that the fields must share the same name but have different export values.

An export value is the information used by a CGI application on a Web server to identify the selected field.

1 If needed, scroll to the bottom of the page to view the credit card section.

2 Select the form tool, and drag a box that surrounds the circle just to the left of the word "Visa."

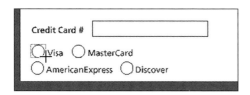

3 For Name, enter **Credit Card**, and for Type, choose Radio Button.

4 Click the Radio Button Options tab. For Radio Style, choose Circle. For Export Value, enter **Visa**.

5 Click the Appearance tab. Deselect Border Color and Background Color. For Width, choose Thin, and for Style, choose Solid. Click OK.

Instead of using the form tool to create the other radio buttons, you'll save time by simply copying the field you just created. When you duplicate a form field, you must remember to edit the appropriate field properties for the new field.

6 Click in a blank area of the form with the form tool to deselect all form fields.

7 Move the pointer inside the Credit Card field you just created, hold down Ctrl (Windows) or Option (Macintosh), and drag the field to the left of the word "MasterCard." Hold down Shift to constrain the duplicate field along the same horizontal or vertical line as the original field.

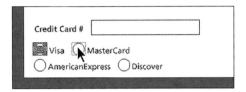

8 Repeat steps 6 and 7 to create fields next to the words "American Express" and "Discover."

9 Double-click the field next to "MasterCard" to open the Field Properties dialog box. Enter **MasterCard** as the export value, and click OK.

10 Repeat step 9 for the fields next to "American Express" and "Discover," assigning the appropriate credit card name as the export value for each field.

11 Select the hand tool, and click inside the newly created radio button fields. Notice that you can only select one item at a time.

Note: If the radio buttons do not line up properly with the original circles in the page, use the form tool to move the fields into position.

Creating a Submit Form data field

To set up a submit button correctly, you specify a Uniform Resource Locator (URL) with the Submit Form action. A CGI application must be on the Web server to collect and route the data to a database. An existing CGI application that collects data from HTML forms can be used to collect data from FDF forms if the field names match those set in the CGI application.

1 Scroll to view the Submit item in the lower right corner of the page.

2 Select the form tool, and drag a box around the Submit item.

3 For Name, enter **Submit**, and for Type, choose Button.

4 Click the Button Options tab. For Highlight, choose None, and for Layout, choose Text only.

5 Click the Appearance tab. Deselect Border Color and Background Color, and for Style, choose Solid.

6 Click the Actions tab. Select Mouse Up, and click Add.

7 For Type, choose Submit Form, and click Select URL.

8 Enter **http://cgi1.adobe.com/acrobat/finalfrm.cgi** as the URL. Under Export Format, click Forms Data Format, and click OK. Click Set Action, and then click OK to add the Submit button.

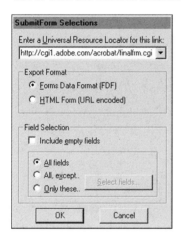

Creating a Reset Form field

You can specify a Reset Form action to clear the data that has already been entered in a form. You might reset a form to clear a mistake, or to clear the form for another user to fill in.

1 Select the form tool, and drag a box around the Reset item in the lower right corner of the form.

2 For Name, enter **Reset**, and for Type, choose Button.

3 Click the Button Options tab. For Highlight, choose None, and for Layout, choose Text only.

4 Click the Appearance tab. Deselect Border Color and Background Color, and for Style, choose Solid.

5 Click the Actions tab. Select Mouse Up, and click Add.

6 For Type, choose Reset Form, and click Select Fields.

7 In the Field Selection dialog box, select All Fields, and click OK. Click Set Action, and then click OK to add the Reset button to the form.

8 Select the hand tool.

Filling out the fields

Now you can experiment with filling out the fields you've just created and resetting the form. All the fields should work properly except for the Submit button. The Submit button would only work if you were viewing this document inside a Web browser and it was directed at a CGI script running on a Web server.

When you are finished experimenting with the form, choose File > Save As, name the file 09work.pdf, and save it in your PROJECTS folder. Then close the file.

Review

You have just learned how to create and use PDF forms. Now you can use your new skills to get your existing and future forms online. Work with your Web administrator to collect the data from those forms and keep your databases up to date.

To test your knowledge of the concepts and techniques you learned in this lesson, answer the following questions:

• What is the difference between a check box and a radio button?

• What is the purpose of a Submit button?

• When will a Submit button send data to a CGI application on a Web server?

• Which fields will populate in a form if you use the Import > Form Data command?

• What is a combo box?

• How do you copy a form field?

B

Project

Multimedia Project

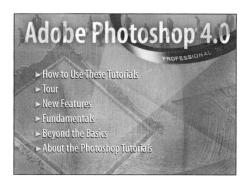

In this project, you will use the skills learned in previous lessons to put together a document that will act as an interface to a software tutorial. You will enhance the file with buttons, movies, actions, and sounds. Take time to experiment, and have fun.

In this project, you will apply the skills you learned in the previous lessons to create a self-guiding tutorial that was designed to be used online. You will do the following:

- Add buttons with multiple actions.
- Add a page action.
- Add a movie.
- Choose the opening view of a document.

This project will take about 50 minutes to complete.

About this multimedia project

The document that you will work with in this project is part of the actual Adobe Photoshop 4.0 tutorial shell. It was created to provide users of the Photoshop tutorial with an interface to the instructional movies and step-by-step lessons.

You will add some of the elements, such as buttons, that exist in the released version of the shell, and also add other elements that do not.

Opening the work file

1 Start Acrobat Exchange.

2 Choose File > Open, locate and select Tutorial.pdf in the Projectb folder, and click Open.

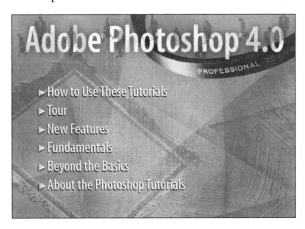

3 Take a moment to page through the document. Notice the "home" button that appears on every page except the first page. This button has a Go to View action assigned to it that always returns the user to the home page.

4 Click the home button to return to the first page.

Adding a Go to View button

The Go to View action allows you to create a button that links to a page other than the first, last, next, or previous page. First, you create a button on the destination page, then duplicate it across the appropriate pages in the document. In some cases, you will delete it from the destination page.

Note: The Go to View action assigned to a button can only be used to jump to a destination within the same file. If you want a button to open another file, use the Open File action.

In this section, you will add a button that goes to the "How to Use These Tutorials" page of the document and then duplicate it across other pages.

1 Go to page 2. This page describes how to use the Photoshop tutorial.

2 Select the form tool (🖳) from the toolbar.

3 Drag to make a box about the same size as and above the Quit button at the bottom of the page.

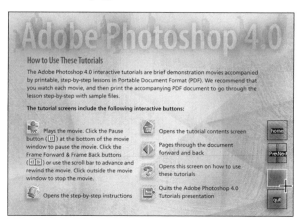

4 In the Name text field, type **How to**, and for Type, select Button.

5 Click the Button Options tab. From the Highlight pop-up menu, select None, and from the Layout pop-up menu, select Icon only.

6 In the Appearance when UP box, click Icon.

7 Click Browse. Locate and select Qustmks.pdf in the Projectb folder, and click OK or Open.

8 Use the scroll bar to view the available question mark styles, select one, and click OK.

9 Click the Appearance tab. Deselect Border Color and Background Color. For Style, select Solid.

10 Click the Actions tab. Select Mouse Up, and click Add.

11 For Type, select Go to View. For Magnification, select Fit View.

12 Click Set Action and OK.

13 Select the hand tool to view the new button.

Note: If you need to resize the button to match the size of the other buttons, select the form tool and the button, then drag a handle to resize the button. Reselect the hand tool after resizing the button.

You have just added a button with an action to show the current view of page 2 when clicked. Next, you will assign another action to occur when the "How to" button is clicked, then duplicate it across the appropriate pages in the document.

Adding multiple actions to a button

You can assign more than one action to a button, and also sort the order in which those actions occur after assigning them.

1 Select the form tool and double-click the "How to" button.

2 Click the Actions tab.

3 Select Mouse Up. Notice that the Go to View action is already listed in the Do the following column.

4 Click Add. For Type, select Sound, and click Select Sound.

5 Locate and select one of the click files—click1.wav, click2.wav, or click3.wav (Windows) or click1.aif, click2.aif, or click3.aif (Macintosh)—from the Projectb folder, then click Open and Set Action.

Now two actions are listed in the Do the following column—Go to View and Sound. When the button is clicked, the actions will activate in the order listed. But for this tutorial we want the user to hear the sound first, then go to the destination view. So, we will reorder the actions.

6 Select the Sound entry in the Do the following column and click Up.

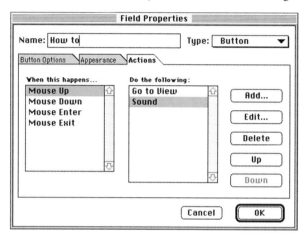

Sound moves up in the list and will now activate before the Go to View action.

7 Click OK.

Duplicating the How to button

Now that you have formatted the How to button, you will duplicate it so that the users of this document can easily access the "How to" information from other pages in the document.

1 Select the How to button with the form tool. You know the button is selected when handles appear in the four corners of the button field.

2 Choose Edit > Fields > Duplicate.

3 Click From, enter pages **2** to **9** in the Duplicate Fields dialog box, and click OK.

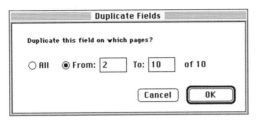

4 Select the hand tool.

5 Go to page 3.

6 Click the How to button.

Notice that you hear the clicking sound, then go to the How to Use These Tutorials page. Duplicating buttons makes it easy to add navigational buttons across multiple pages.

7 Choose File > Save As. Save the file as Projectb.pdf in the Projectb folder.

Note: Because there are links to movies in this file, you need to save this file in the Projectb folder to maintain the relative relationship between the PDF file and the movie files. If the relative file relationship is not maintained, you will receive an error message and the movies will not play when activated by an action or clicked.

Adding more buttons and page actions

To add some interesting effects to this shell, you will add more buttons and page actions, and then combine them to get the final effect. First, you will watch how combining buttons and page actions can work together.

1 Go to page 3.

2 Move your pointer over the arrow ▶ just to the left of the words "Shutter Effects". Notice that an image appears, and a sound plays.

3 Move your pointer away from the arrow, and the image disappears. The arrow icon has Show-Hide Field and Sound actions assigned to it.

4 Now click the Shutter Effects link to go to that topic. When the page opens, a short movie plays, then stops.

5 Click the Go Back button.

In the next section, you will edit this file so that the Shadows topic has the same multimedia effects as the Shutter Effects topic does.

Adding more buttons with multiple actions

Showing and hiding buttons can be a tricky procedure, but once mastered, it can add interest to any multimedia project. For example, if you do not want to clutter your page with images, but want to entice your users with previews, you can choose to hide the images until you anticipate a user would actually want to see them.

To add the image preview button:

1 Select the form tool from the toolbar.

2 Drag to make a rectangle in an open area on the page that is approximately the same size as the "Mouse" field. After you have formatted this new field, you will move it on top of the "Mouse" field so that the image you are adding appears in the same place as the Shutter Effects image when activated.

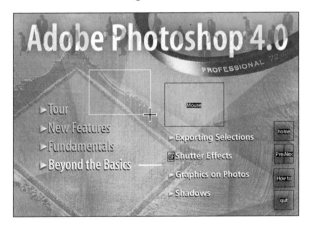

3 In the Name text field, type **Sun**. For Type, select Button.

4 Click the Button Options tab. From the Highlight pop-up menu, select Push. From the Layout pop-up menu, select Icon only.

5 In the Appearance when UP box, click Icon.

6 Click Browse. Locate and select Shadow.pdf from the list of files in the Projectb folder, and click OK or Open, then click OK again. Shadow.pdf is the image preview for the Shadows topic.

7 Click the Appearance tab. Deselect Border Color and Background Color. For Style, select Solid.

8 Click OK.

9 Drag the "Sun" field on top of the "Mouse" field.

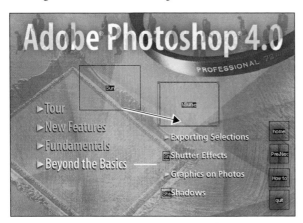

Now you will add another button field that will show and hide the Sun button, as well as play a sound.

To add the arrow button:

1 Drag to make a rectangle around the arrow 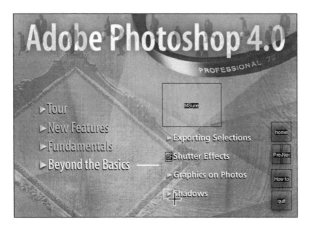 just to the left of the word "Shadows".

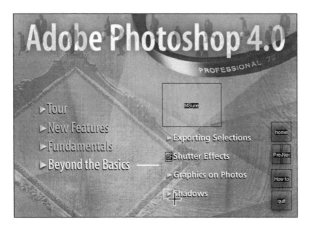

2 In the Name text field, enter **Shadows**. For Type, select Button.

This field will be represented by the image of the arrow on the page, so you do not need to set Button or Appearance options.

3 Click the Actions tab.

4 Select Mouse Enter, and click Add.

5 For Type, select Show-Hide Field, and click Edit.

6 Click Show, and select Sun.

7 Click OK and Set Action.

Now you will add a sound to play.

8 Click Add. For Type, select Sound, and click Select Sound.

9 Select Shadow.wav (Windows) or Shadow.aif (Macintosh), then click Open and Set Action.

Now you need to assign an action to hide the image on Mouse Exit.

10 Select Mouse Exit, and click Add.

11 For Type, select Show-Hide Field, and click Edit.

12 Click Hide, select Sun, and click OK.

13 Click Set Action and OK to close the Field Properties dialog box.

14 Select the hand tool and drag it over the arrow just to the left of the word "Shadows", and then away from the arrow to see the effect.

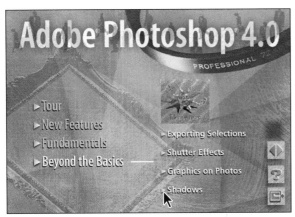

Arrow over the Show-Hide field, the graphic is displayed and sound is played

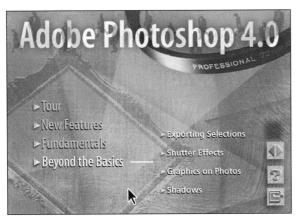

Arrow away from the Show-Hide field and graphic is hidden

15 Click the Shadows link to go to that topic.

You will now add a movie to this page that will play automatically when the page opens.

To add a movie:

1 Select the movie tool from the toolbar.

2 Click once in the center of the sun image.

3 Locate and select Shadow2.mov from the list of files in the Projectb folder, and click OK or Open.

4 For Title, enter **Shadow2**. For Movie Poster, choose Don't Show Poster.

5 Under Player Options, deselect Show Controller. For Mode, choose Play Once then Stop. If needed, deselect Floating Window (Windows) or Use Floating Window (Macintosh).

6 Under Border Appearance, for Width, select Invisible.

7 Click OK.

8 Select the hand tool.

9 Choose Document > Set Page Action.

10 Select Page Open, and click Add.

11 For Type, select Movie, and click Select Movie.

12 For Select Movie, choose Shadow2. For Select Operation, choose Play.

13 Click OK, Set Action, and OK.

Now let's try it out.

14 Click the Go Back button.

15 Move the pointer over the arrow to the left of the word "Shadows" to see the effect you added earlier again.

16 Click the Shadows link. The short movie plays immediately after the page opens.

17 Choose File > Save As. Name the file Project2.pdf, and save it in the Projectb folder.

Choosing the opening view

The opening view of a document should be determined by the file's purpose, audience, and design. The actual Photoshop 4.0 tutorial shell was designed to teach users how to use Photoshop, not Acrobat. To focus the users on the content of the shell rather than on the program running it, the designers of the Photoshop shell decided to limit the window elements that a Photoshop user could interact with. In this section, you will learn how to choose opening view options, and see the effects of those choices.

1 Choose File > Document Info > Open.

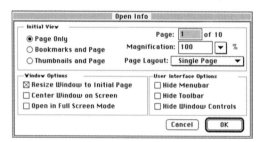

2 Select the following options:

• Resize Window to Initial Page

• Center Window on Screen

• Hide Toolbar

• Hide Window Controls

3 Click OK.

4 Choose File > Save As. Save the file as Project3.pdf, and save it in the Projectb folder.

Because the changes only take effect when you open the file, you must close it and reopen it to see the changes.

5 Choose File > Close.

6 Choose File > Open. Open Project3.pdf.

7 Notice the changes in the opening view of the file.

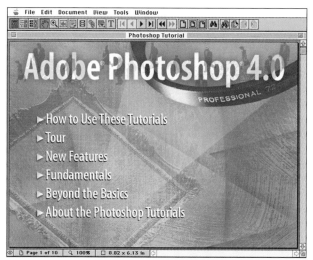

Opening view with all elements enabled

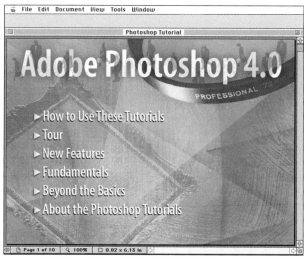

Opening view with limited elements

Adding quit and go back buttons

To further distance a document from the program running it, you can disable the menu bar. But if you disable the menu bar, you need to add buttons that allow users to quit the file they are reading.

To add a quit button:

1 Press the Right Arrow key on your keyboard.

2 Click the Quit button

3 Choose Window > Show Toolbar.

4 Select the form tool from the toolbar.

5 Draw a box around the Yes box on the page.

6 Type **Yes** in the Name text field, and select Button as Type.

7 Click the Actions tab. Select Mouse Up, and click Add.

8 Choose Execute Menu Item, and click Edit Menu Item.

9 In the Menu Item Selection window, choose File > Exit (Windows) or File > Quit (Macintosh), then click OK, Set Action, and OK.

To add a go back button:

1 Draw a box around the No box on the page.

2 Type **No** in the Name text field, and select Button as Type.

3 Click the Actions tab. Select Mouse Up, and click Add.

4 Choose Execute Menu Item, and click Edit Menu Item.

5 In the Menu Item Selection window, choose View > Go Back, then click OK, Set Action, and OK.

Hiding the menu bar

1 Choose File > Document Info > Open.

2 Select Hide Menu bar, and click OK.

3 Choose File Save As. Save the file as Project3.pdf, and replace the existing file.

4 Select the hand tool.

5 Choose File > Close.

6 Choose File > Open and reopen Project3.pdf. Notice that the menu bar is now hidden.

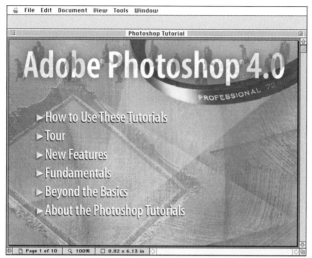

View with menu bars visible

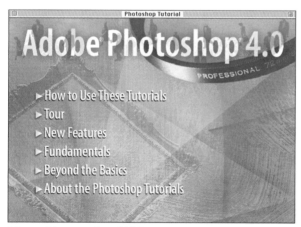

View with menu bars hidden

7 Click the Beyond the Basics link.

8 Click the Quit button.

9 Click No. You return to the Beyond the Basics page.

10 Click the Quit button again. This time click Yes. You quit out of Exchange.

Review

Take some time to experiment with the actions that you can assign to buttons, links, bookmarks, and pages. You may find that actions add a new level of communication possibilities and fun to your PDF documents that you never thought possible before.

To test your knowledge of the concepts and techniques you learned in this lesson, answer the following questions:

• How do you create a button on page 6 with Go to View action that points at page 17?

• When selected, what does the Hidden option on the Appearance tab of the Field Properties dialog box do?

• What actions can you assign to a button?

• What other types of elements can you assign actions to?

• What happens to the display of a movie when you choose floating window as an option in your Movie Properties dialog box?

• Is there a way to display the menu bar or toolbar if they are hidden from view? [Hint: You may have to look in the online guide for the answer.]

10

Lesson 10

Using Exchange in a Document Review Cycle

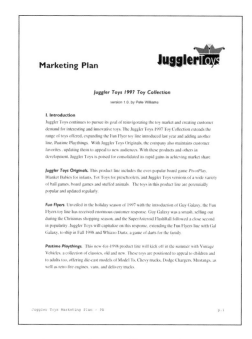

Acrobat can play an effective role in a document review cycle, where a single document is distributed to an audience of reviewers. By circulating a PDF document, you can receive comments back in the form of notes–electronic "stickies" attached to the file. You can then collate the notes and compile them in a single file for easier viewing.

In this lesson, you'll learn how to do the following:

- Use and create notes.
- Import, export, and summarize notes.
- Import a TIFF image file (Windows only).
- Capture a PDF Image file (Windows only).
- Show and correct Capture suspects (Windows only).
- Set file security settings.
- View security information for a document.

This lesson will take about 30 minutes to complete.

Opening the work file

In this lesson, you'll work with a marketing plan document for Juggler Toys Company. This document is at an intermediate draft stage, and some of the marketing strategies are still being developed. You'll gather a variety of review comments and memos about the current marketing plan and attach them electronically to the document draft.

1 Start Acrobat Exchange.

2 Choose File > Open. Select Mktplan.pdf, located in the Lesson10 folder, and click Open.

Using notes

Acrobat's notes feature lets you attach short text messages to an existing document. With notes, multiple reviewers can comment on and incorporate their comments in the same review version. Notes from other document versions can also be collected and incorporated into the review version.

Reviewing notes

1 If needed, click the Fit Page button to view the first page of the marketing plan. Notice the different-colored notes that appear in the margins.

2 Using the hand tool, double-click a note to read it. Click the close box at the top of the note window when you have finished reading it.

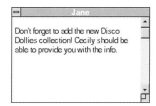

3 Double-click a note of a different color to read it. Notice that the note's label is different from the previous note.

Notes can be set to different colors to indicate that they were written by different reviewers.

4 Close the note when you have finished viewing it.

You can move notes around easily on a page.

5 Using the hand tool, drag the blue note to the left margin.

Importing notes

The current document includes notes from several different reviewers. However, another reviewer has placed her comments in a different copy of the marketing plan. You'll import the notes from this reviewer into the first document version.

1 Choose File > Import > Notes.

2 Select Review.pdf, located in the Lesson10 folder, and click Select.

3 Page through the marketing plan document and notice the new magenta notes that have been imported.

You'll add your own note to this compiled document using the notes tool. But first you'll customize your note style by setting preferences.

Setting note preferences

1 Choose File > Preferences > Notes.

The Note Preferences dialog box appears.

2 For Default Label, enter your name.

3 For Default Color, choose Red.

When you transfer a note between different files or systems, the label and color of the note are preserved.

You can also specify a font for displaying the note text. However, keep in mind that this font preference applies only to your system; users viewing your note on other systems may see a different font, depending on their own preference setting.

4 For Font, choose Helvetica, and enter 12 for the point size. Then click OK.

Creating a new note

You use the notes tool in Exchange to create notes of your own using the style preferences you've just specified. Although you can view notes in a PDF file using Acrobat Reader, you can only create or edit notes using Exchange.

1 If needed, go to page 1, and click the notes tool (📝) in the toolbar.

When you move the pointer over the page, the pointer appears as a set of cross hairs.

2 Click in the page below the final paragraph.

An empty note window appears.

3 Type the following phrase: **Do Disco Dollies come with accessories?** Then close the note window.

4 Double-click the note you've just created to view the message. Close the note when you are finished.

Deleting a note

You can easily delete unwanted notes from a document.

1 Click the hand tool, and click the green note on page 1 to select it.

2 Press Delete, and click OK to the confirmation message.

Exporting notes

You can export just the notes from a document and place them in a new PDF file.

1 Choose File > Export > Notes.

2 Name the file Comments.pdf, and save it in your PROJECTS folder.

3 Choose File > Open. Select Comments.pdf and click Open. Then click Fit Page.

4 Choose Window > Tile Vertically to display the two documents side by side.

Notice that the Comments.pdf file contains the exported notes in their original placements on the page. Because the file contains only the notes, it is smaller in size than the original file and therefore more economical to distribute.

5 Close the Comments.pdf file when you are finished viewing it, and resize the Mktplan.pdf window.

Summarizing notes

At times you may want to display just the text of notes so that you don't have to open each note individually to read it. By summarizing notes, you can compile all the text in a set of notes into a new PDF document.

1 Choose Tools > Summarize Notes.

A new PDF file is created. This document lists the notes that appear on each page of the marketing plan, including the note labels, the dates they were added to the file, and the full text of the notes.

2 Choose File > Save As. Name the file Notes.pdf and save it in your PROJECTS folder.

3 Close Notes.pdf when you are finished viewing it.

Now you'll append the summarized notes to the marketing plan review.

4 Choose Document > Insert Pages.

5 Select Notes.pdf, located in the PROJECTS folder, and click Select.

6 For Location, click After. For Page, click Last. Then click OK to insert the summarized notes into the review version of the marketing plan.

7 Choose File > Save As, name the file 10work.pdf, and save it in your PROJECTS folder.

If you are using Acrobat for Windows, you can go on to the next section, "Capturing a fax image file." If you are using a Macintosh, skip to "Setting file security" on page 243.

Capturing a fax image file (Windows only)

You can use the Import feature to convert image files, such as TIFF images or scanned paper documents, to PDF pages. When you import an image, all the elements in the original image remain as bitmap pictures in the PDF page. If your imported image contains text, you may want to use the Capture feature to convert the bitmap text to text that can be edited and searched in Acrobat Exchange.

One reviewer of the marketing plan has faxed in a memo containing her comments. We've scanned the fax and saved it as a TIFF image file for you to import and capture.

Importing the fax

1 Choose File > Import > Image.

2 Select Fax.tif, located in the Lesson10 folder, and click Open.

3 Select Create New Document, and click OK.

The fax image file is imported as a new PDF document.

4 Click the touch-up tool (**T**) and click in the fax text.

Notice that you cannot edit the text in the document. The TIFF file has been imported as a PDF Image file; that is, all elements in the document, including the text, are basically pictures that can't be edited.

You'll convert the file to PDF Normal format using the Capture Pages command. A PDF Normal document contains editable text that can be altered, scaled, and reformatted as desired.

Capturing the fax image

1 Choose Document > Capture Pages.

You can restrict which pages of the document you want to capture and specify preference settings for Capture.

2 Click Current Page to capture the page currently displayed on-screen.

3 Click Preferences. In the Preferences dialog box, choose English (US) for the language and Normal for the style.

You can capture a file as a PDF Normal file, or you can have Acrobat display the original text images with the converted text hidden beneath.

4 Click OK to exit the Preferences dialog box, and click OK again to capture the fax document.

5 Click the touch-up text tool (**T**) and click in the document. Notice that you can now edit the text.

Cropping the file

Now you'll crop the captured file to a standard page size.

Note: You must capture a file before cropping or rotating it. If you capture a file after you crop or rotate it, you will lose the changes you have made to the file.

1 Click the Fit Page button.

Look at the page status bar. Notice that the page size is 9 inches by 11 inches. You'll crop the page to standard letter size, 8.5 inches by 11 inches.

2 Choose Document > Crop Pages.

3 In the Crop Pages dialog box, enter **0.25** for both Left and Right, and click OK. Click OK again to the confirmation message that appears.

Correcting suspects (Windows only)

The Capture feature converts a bitmap text image into its equivalent text characters. If Capture suspects that it has not recognized a word correctly, it displays the bitmap image for the word in the document and hides its best guess for the word behind the bitmap. You can view these *suspect* words in the captured document.

Showing suspects

Choose Edit > Show Capture Suspects.

The suspect words appear highlighted in the document. Next, you'll examine each suspect and correct or accept Capture's best guess for the word.

Correcting suspects

1 Select the zoom tool and drag to magnify the first suspect in the first line of the memo.

2 Choose Edit > Find First Suspect.

The original bitmap word appears enlarged in the Capture Suspect window. In the document, notice that Capture has substituted the wrong characters for this ambiguous word.

 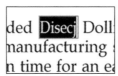

You can correct a suspect word by typing in the desired characters, or you can accept Capture's best guess for the word. Since Capture's guess is obviously wrong, you'll type in the correct word.

3 Type **Disco** on the keyboard. Notice that the word is updated in the document as you type. Then click Accept to convert the image text to the word you just typed.

The first suspect is converted to editable text, and the Capture Suspect window shows the next suspect word, "day-glo."

4 Click Accept to convert the bitmap text to Capture's best approximation for the word.

5 Click Accept again to correct the final suspect.

6 Choose File > Save As. Name the file Fax.pdf and save it in your PROJECTS folder. Then close the file.

Combining documents

Now you'll attach this captured memo to the marketing plan document.

1 If needed, make 10work.pdf the active document.

2 Choose Document > Insert Pages. Select Fax.pdf, located in the Lesson 10 folder, and click Select.

3 For Location, click Before. For Page, click First. Then click OK.

4 Choose File > Save As, and save 10work.pdf in your Lesson 10 folder. You can replace the existing 10work.pdf.

Setting file security

Sometimes you may want to lock a PDF document to prevent it from being edited. For example, now that you've gathered all the review comments for the Juggler Toys marketing plan, you'll want to protect the compiled file from accidental changes.

Setting file security

1 Choose File > Save As.

2 Click Security.

The Security dialog box appears. You can specify up to two passwords—one for opening the file, and one for applying changes to the file. These passwords are case-sensitive.

3 For Open the Document, enter **Circus**, and press Tab.

4 For Change Security Options, enter **ferris**.

5 For Do Not Allow, select Changing the Document, Selecting Text and Graphics, and Adding or Changing Notes and Form Fields. Then click OK.

A dialog box appears asking you to confirm your Open password.

6 Type **Circus** and click OK.

Another dialog box appears asking you to confirm your Security password.

7 Type **ferris** and click OK.

8 Name the document 10work2.pdf, and save it in your PROJECTS folder. Then close the document.

Testing file security

1 Choose File > Open. Select 10work2.pdf, located in the PROJECTS folder, and click Open.

A dialog box appears asking you for the Open password.

2 Enter the password and click OK.

3 Notice that the commands under the Edit and Document menus are dimmed, indicating that you cannot modify the document pages. Notice also that most of the tools in the toolbar are dimmed.

4 Choose File > Document Info > Security.

The Security Info dialog box summarizes the security settings that have been placed on the document. Notice that the document has both Open and Security passwords, and that no actions except printing the document are allowed.

5 Click OK when you are finished viewing the information.

6 Click File > Save As and click Security.

A dialog box appears asking you for the Security password.

7 Enter the password and click OK.

8 Under Do Not Allow, deselect Selecting Text and Graphics, and click OK. Then click Save, and click Yes to the confirmation message.

9 Click the touch-up tool and notice that you can now select text in the document.

10 Close 10work2.pdf. You do not need to save your changes.

Review

In this lesson, you've learned how to create and use notes, and how to assign security settings to a file. If you were using Acrobat for Windows, you also learned how to capture an image file and correct text that was captured incorrectly.

To test your knowledge of the concepts and techniques you learned in this lesson, answer the following questions:

• How do you change the label and color of a note?

• What font is used in a note when viewed on your computer? On someone else's computer?

• How do you create a file that contains only the labels, times, dates, and content of all notes added to a PDF file?

- What types of image files can you import into Exchange?
- What are the characteristics of a PDF Image file?
- What is a "suspect" word?
- What types of security passwords can you assign to a document?

11

Lesson 11

Building a Searchable PDF Library

Converting all of your electronic and paper publications to PDF lets you distribute and search large collections of documents quickly and easily. You can use Acrobat Catalog to create a full-text index of your PDF publications, and then use the Search command in Exchange or Reader to search the entire library almost instantly.

In this lesson, you will learn how to do the following:

• Build an index using Acrobat Catalog.

• Use the Search command to locate information contained in the files indexed by Catalog.

• Set Search options.

• Refine a search.

• Use Document Info fields to conduct a search.

• Search for information using Boolean expressions.

This lesson will take about 30 minutes to complete.

Note: In order to complete the steps in this lesson, you must copy the Lesson11 folder to your hard drive, not to your desktop.

Building an index

You use Acrobat Catalog to build full-text indexes of PDF document collections. A full-text index is a searchable database of all the text in a document or set of documents. Your documents should be complete in content and electronic features such as links, bookmarks, and form fields before you use Catalog to index them. In this lesson, you'll work with chapter files from the book, *Hawaii: The Big Island Revealed*, by Andrew Doughty and Harriett Friedman.

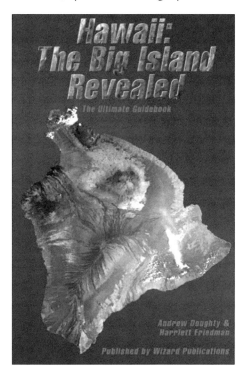

You will create an index of these files and then search that index to find exciting information about what to do on your next trip to Hawaii.

1 In Windows Explorer (Windows) or in the Finder (Macintosh), open the Hawaii folder, located inside the Lesson11 folder. Notice the files contained within this folder. All of the PDF files in this folder will be indexed by Catalog.

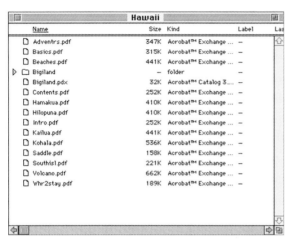

2 Start Acrobat Catalog.

3 If you are using a Macintosh, choose Edit > Preferences, deselect Make include/exclude folders DOS compatible, and click OK.

4 Choose Index > New (Windows) or File > New (Macintosh). For Index Title, enter **Hawaii: The Big Island.**

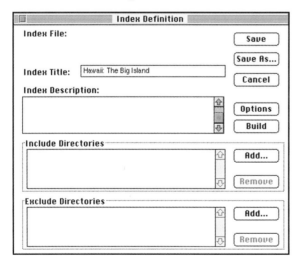

The Index Description box provides users with more information about the documents included in the index.

5 Click inside the Index Description box, and enter the following information about the index you are building: **The Ultimate Guidebook. The most comprehensive, yet easy to use guidebook ever written for the Big Island.**

6 Under Include Directories, click Add.

Now you will select the folder or folders that contain the documents to be indexed.

7 Do one of the following:

• In Windows, double-click to select the Hawaii folder located inside the Lesson11 folder, and click OK.

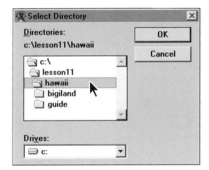

• On the Macintosh, click to select the Hawaii folder located inside the Lesson11 folder and click Select "Hawaii".

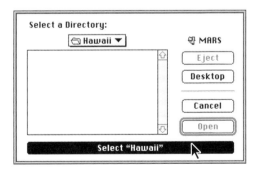

By default, Catalog indexes subdirectories, but you can exclude subdirectories using the Exclude Directories option. You can also add more than one directory to the index. For this lesson you will index one directory.

8 Click Build.

9 Name the index Guide.pdx, open the Hawaii folder as the save location, and click OK (Windows) or Save (Macintosh). The file extension PDX identifies a file as an Acrobat index.

10 Quit Catalog after "Index Build Successful" appears in the Catalog message window.

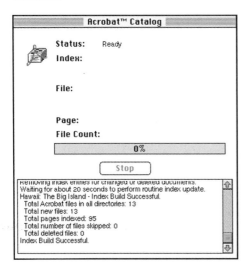

For information about index options and scheduling index builds, see the *Catalog Online Guide.*

Searching an index

Now you'll use the Search command in Exchange to perform searches of the PDF documents you just indexed with Catalog. You will also use the Search command to limit and expand the definition of the term for which you are searching.

By searching a full-text index, you can quickly search a collection of PDF documents; by contrast, the find tool (see page 21) works only with a single PDF document and reads every word on every page, a much slower process.

1 Start Acrobat Exchange.

2 Click the Search button (⚲) in the toolbar to open the Search dialog box.

First you will select an index to search.

3 Click Indexes to display the Index Selection dialog box.

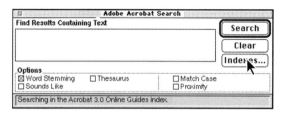

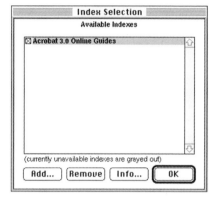

4 Click Add.

5 Locate the Hawaii folder inside the Lesson11 folder, and click Open.

6 Select Guide.pdx inside the Hawaii folder, and click OK (Windows) or Open (Macintosh).

The Hawaii: The Big Island index now appears under the list of available indexes.

7 If needed, click the boxes next to the other indexes in the list to deselect them. Then click OK.

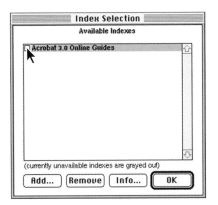

Acrobat searches only the selected index or indexes in the Available Indexes list. Here, you will search only for entries in the Hawaii index.

To find information contained in the Hawaii index, you enter a word or phrase representing the desired topic.

8 Under Find Results Containing Text, enter **hiking**.

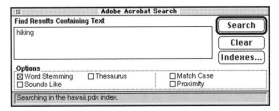

9 Under Options, select Word Stemming, and deselect all other search options.

The Word Stemming option tells Search to look also for words that share the same word stem as "hiking," such as "hike" or "hiked." For detailed information on each of the search options, see the *Search Online Guide.*

10 Click Search.

Looking at the Search Results list

The Search Results window lists the documents that contain the word or words you searched for. The list also tells you how many documents were searched and how many were found to contain the words. In this example, 13 documents were searched, with 11 containing variations of the word "hiking."

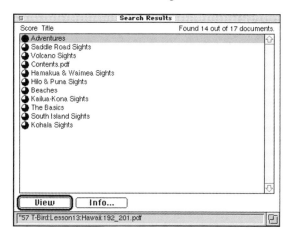

The documents are listed by relative ranking—documents with solid circles have more occurrences of the search words relative to the other documents in the list.

Acrobat Search uses five icons to indicate a document's relevance ranking:

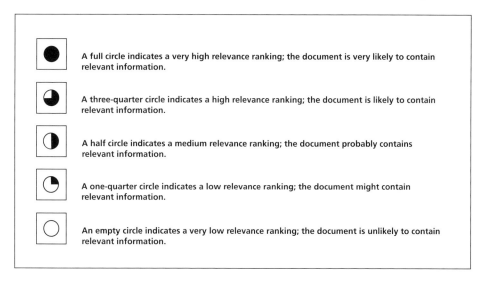

If needed, use the scroll bar or resize the Search Results window to view the entire list. You can open any of the documents in the list and view the highlighted search words.

1 Select the Adventures entry at the top of the list, and click View to display the corresponding document. If needed, click the Fit Page button to view the entire document page.

Notice the highlighted occurrences of the word "hike." Since the Adventures document contains many occurrences of the searched word, it is ranked near the top of the Search Results list. If desired, use the zoom tool to magnify a section in which "hike" is highlighted.

2 Click the Search Results button (⬛) to redisplay the Search Results list.

3 Double-click Kohala Sights to open that document. If needed, click the Fit Page button to view the highlighted occurrence of "hiking."

The Kohala Sights document is ranked at the bottom of the Search Results list because it has fewer occurrences of the searched word than the other files in the list.

4 Choose File > Close to close the document.

Narrowing the search

To make searching more effective, you should define your search criteria as much as possible. So far, you have found 11 documents that contain some information about hiking on the island of Hawaii. Now you will refine your search to list only those documents that contain information about hiking near volcanoes.

1 Click the Search button.

2 Under Find Results Containing Text, after "hiking," enter the words **and volcanoes**.

3 Under Options, deselect Word Stemming to search only for the specific words you entered.

You are about to do a refined search. A refined search tells Search to look only at the documents in your current results list and to apply the new search criteria (instead of searching the index completely from scratch).

4 Hold down Ctrl (Windows) or Option (Macintosh) to change the Search button to Refine, and click Refine.

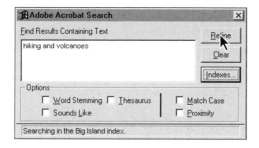

Notice that 6 documents out of the 11 in the last Search Results list meet the new search criteria. Using very specific search criteria helps you quickly identify which documents, if any, contain the information you are looking for.

Notice that you have eliminated 5 documents with this search, but that the ranking of the remaining 6 documents is very close.

Affecting the ranking order

You need to know which, if any, of the 6 listed documents is the best candidate for information about hiking near volcanoes. You can affect the relative ranking order by using any of the options displayed in the Adobe Acrobat Search dialog box.

1 Click the Search button in the toolbar.

2 Under Options, select Proximity.

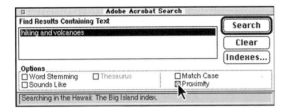

The Proximity option tells Search to find documents in which the search words occur within three pages of each other. If the words are more than three pages apart, the document fails the search criteria and will not be listed in the Search Results window.

3 Hold down Ctrl (Windows) or Option (Macintosh) to make the Search button change to Refine, and click Refine.

Notice that the Search Results list has narrowed the field to 3 documents with very different relative rankings.

4 Select Volcano Sights in the list, and click View. If needed, click the Fit Page button to view the whole document page.

Notice that nearby occurrences of "hiking" and "volcano" are highlighted. If desired, zoom in on the highlighted text to read the information.

5 Choose File > Close to close the document.

Using Document Info fields to search

In addition to conducting a search based on specific words, you can search a collection of documents using any one of the Document Info fields. In this section, you will search for documents that have a specific entry in their Subject fields.

First, you will make sure that the Adobe Acrobat Search dialog box displays Document Info fields.

1 Choose File > Preferences > Search to display the Search Preferences dialog box.

2 Under Query, select Show Fields if needed, and click OK.

3 Click the Search button in the toolbar.

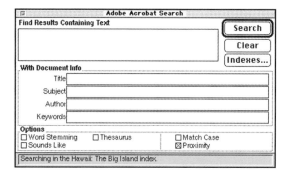

Notice that the Adobe Acrobat Search dialog box now includes an area for you to search in the Document Info fields.

The Title, Subject, and Keywords for the documents in the Hawaii index have been added to help you search them. Adobe recommends adding this information to any PDF files you create to make searching more efficient.

4 Click Clear to clear the text and Document Info fields.

5 For Subject, enter **beaches**, and click Search.

Notice that you found 3 documents that meet the search criteria.

6 Double-click Beaches to open that document. If needed, click the Fit Page button to view the whole page.

7 Click the Search Next (🖹) button to open the next document in the Search Results list. Once you click the Search Next button, the Search Previous (🖹) button becomes available. You use the Search Next and Search Previous buttons to browse through a Search Results list.

Note: If you are unable to access the Search Next and Search Previous buttons from the toolbar, use the commands found under Tools > Search.

8 Choose File > Close to close the current document.

Searching with Boolean expressions

You can use AND, OR, and NOT operators to build a logical expression (called a *Boolean expression*) that searches for words in a specific relation to each other. For example, earlier in this lesson you used the AND operator to build an expression that searched for occurrences of both "hiking" and "volcanoes" in the same document.

Using the OR operator

Use OR to find documents containing any of two or more search terms. Maybe you aren't sure what you want to do one day on your vacation—you could go diving or to Kailua.

1 Click the Search button in the toolbar.

2 Click Clear to clear the text and Document Info fields. Deselect all search options.

3 Under Find Results Containing Text, enter **diving or Kailua.**

4 Click Search.

The Search Results window lists 9 documents that contain information about either diving or Kailua. You can open any of the documents to find information about one subject or the other, but not necessarily both.

Using the AND operator

If you plan it right, you might be able to go diving and see Kailua in one day trip. Use AND to find documents containing two or more search terms.

1 Click the Search button in the toolbar.

2 Click Clear. Under Find Results Containing Text, enter **diving and Kailua.**

3 Click Search.

Three documents contain information about both diving and Kailua.

4 Double-click Beaches to open that document. Zoom in on the bottom right quarter of the page to learn about a small cove near Kailua that is excellent for scuba diving.

You can also search with the NOT Boolean operator, combine Boolean operators, and search with wild-card characters. See the *Search Online Guide* for more information and examples.

5 Close any open files.

Searching on the Web

To locate information in PDF files stored on the Internet or an intranet, you must first set up search-engine software that can search PDF files on your Web server. Users can then run a search from your Web page.

Many companies develop search engines that can automatically and continuously update a search index of both PDF and HTML documents on a Web server. For a current list of these companies, see the Acrobat Web Page at http://www.adobe.com/acrobat/moreinfo.

Review

In this lesson, you learned how to create an index with Acrobat Catalog and how to search an index with the Search command in Exchange (also available in Reader). Adobe recommends that you include an index on CD-ROMs that contain PDF files to help your users access your information with ease and efficiency.

To test your knowledge of the concepts and techniques you learned in this lesson, answer the following questions:

• How can you distinguish an index file from a PDF file?

• What does the Search Results list display?

- How does the Word Stemming option expand your search results?

- What key do you press to do a refined search?

- Why should you enter Document Info field information in all your PDF documents?

- Give two examples of Boolean expressions and what they do.

C

Project

Distributing PDF Documents

Platform independence and small file sizes make PDF an attractive format in which to distribute your documents on the Web, an intranet, or a CD-ROM. In this lesson, you will put the finishing touches on a collection of documents to finalize them for electronic distribution.

In this project, you will learn how to do the following:

- Examine the issues associated with distributing PDF documents.

- Collect documents for distribution.

- Compare image quality and file size between two PDF documents.

- Examine sample *Welcome* documents.

- Add links to a *Welcome* document.

- Add document information to a PDF document.

- Index a document collection with Acrobat Catalog.

- Test PDF documents in a staging area.

- Examine a Web server administrator's checklist.

- This project will take about 30 minutes to complete.

Distributing PDF documents

PDF's ability to faithfully maintain the formatting of a document while offering smaller file sizes, searchable text, printability, and integration with the most popular Web browsers makes it a popular choice for distributing documents on the Web, company intranets, CD-ROMs, and via e-mail. Of course, you could simply create your PDF documents and send them out to the world without any more effort than printing. But with a little extra effort, you could make the information in your documents more accessible to your users and, therefore, more successful documents.

Collecting the documents to publish

The first step is to create or collect your PDF documents. The content of your documents should be complete, and you should be at the point where you would normally print the final copy of those documents.

In this project, you will use the documents you saved in the PROJECTS folder to prepare, arrange, stage, and test for distribution.

Preparing your documents

The content of the documents you are going to use can be assumed to be complete. But there are a few things that must be checked—image quality, file size, and file-names.

Checking image quality and file size

Making bitmap images small enough for network distribution or for mass storage on CD-ROMs generally requires compression—saving images in a way that uses less disk space.

For continuous-tone images such as photographs, JPEG Medium compression (the Distiller and PDF Writer default) saves a lot of space with little loss of quality. You can choose different compression settings to fine-tune the balance between image quality and file size.

In this section of the project, you will open a sample document to view an image that has had no compression applied to it, then choose a compression setting in Distiller and process the PostScript version of that image. You will then compare the image quality and file size of the original file with the compressed file.

1 Start Acrobat Exchange.

2 Choose File > Open, locate and select Drums.pdf in the Projectc folder, and click Open.

3 Click the 400% button in the lower right corner.

Examine the image of the drummer. No compression was applied to this file when it was converted to PDF. Now you will choose a compression setting in Distiller and convert the PostScript version of this file to PDF again.

Choosing a compression setting

1 Start Acrobat Distiller.

2 Choose Distiller > Job Options, and click the General tab. If it is not already selected, for Compatibility choose Acrobat 3.0.

See the *Distiller Online Guide* for information about compatibility settings.

3 Click the Compression tab.

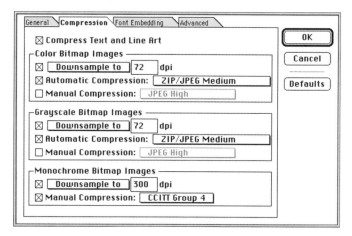

4 In the Color Bitmap Images section, deselect Downsample to.

5 Select Automatic Compression: ZIP/JPEG Medium.

6 Click OK.

The Automatic Compression option determines the best compression method for color and grayscale bitmap images (JPEG, ZIP, or LZW) and applies the correct setting. For example, JPEG compression is used for images with smooth color changes, such as scanned photographs. ZIP (3.0 compatibility) or LZW (2.1. compatibility) compression is used for images with sharp color changes, such as screenshots of dialog boxes.

The image in this file has smooth color changes, therefore, JPEG Medium will be applied to this image.

For more information about compression settings, see the *Distiller Online Guide.*

7 Choose File > Open, locate and select Drumsmed.ps in the Projectc folder, and click Open.

8 Name the file Drumsmed.pdf, save it in the PROJECTS folder, and click OK or Save.

The file is converted to PDF and saved in the PROJECTS folder.

9 Choose Distiller > Job Options. Click the Defaults button, then click OK.

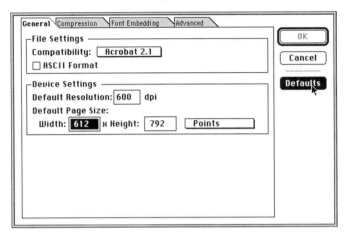

10 Exit or Quit Acrobat Distiller.

Comparing the files in Exchange

1 Return to Acrobat Exchange.

2 Choose File > Open, locate and select Drumsmed.pdf in the PROJECTS folder, and click Open.

3 Choose Window > Tile Vertically. (Only Drums.pdf and Drumsmed.pdf should be open. If other files are open, close them, and choose Window > Tile Vertically again.)

4 Choose 400% magnification from the status bar in the Drumsmed.pdf document. Adjust your viewing area to view the same portion of the image in each file.

As you can see, it is very difficult to detect any quality degradation in the Drumsmed.pdf file that had the default compression applied to it. But, where you will see a significant difference is in the file size—Drums.pdf is 1.4 MB and Drumsmed.pdf is 99K.

5 When you are finished viewing the files, choose Window > Close All.

Comparing compression option results

The compression settings should be determined when you are first creating your PDF documents with Distiller or PDF Writer. For the majority of PDF files, the default compression settings will produce acceptable image quality and file sizes, even with downsampling on. In this section we have provided you with a file to visualize the effect some of the compression options and downsampling had on two sample files and a chart to help you visualize the impact file size can have on file transmission.

Kb: kilobits KB: kilobytes	Data rate (Kb/KB per sec)	60 KB page	300 KB page	10 MB movie
Telephone line	14.4/1.8	34 seconds	3 minutes	1.6 hours
Telephone line	28.8	17 seconds	1.4 minutes	48 minutes
ISDN service	64/7.8	8 seconds	39 seconds	22 minutes
ISDN service	128/15.6	4 seconds	19 seconds	11 minutes
T1 line	1540/188	<1 second	1.6 seconds	54 seconds
T3 line	45000/5500	<1 second	<1 second	1.8 seconds

These numbers represent ideal conditions—use only for comparison. Actual rates vary widely due to many factors. See your telecom provider for availability of lines and services.

Although we do not discuss compression options specifically in this project, in the future you may find a need for more precise control over the compression of your images, and you should use Distiller to process those jobs. PDF Writer does not offer as much control over compression and downsampling as Distiller does. See the *Distiller Online Guide* and *PDF Writer Online Guide* for specific instructions.

Viewing the example file

To give you an idea of the effect a particular compression setting will have on an image, we have supplied you with an example file that contains a series of images converted to PDF with Distiller using various compression and downsampling settings.

1 In Exchange, choose File > Open. Locate and select Imagcomp.pdf from the list of files in the Projectc folder, and click Open.

2 Take some time to zoom in on the images and compare them to each other. The compression and downsampling settings used to process the image are listed beside each image. The file size listed indicates the size of the file if it had existed as its own PDF file.

3 Page through the document to see the effects of compression and downsampling on 300 dpi and 72 dpi color and grayscale images. Continue to zoom in on the images to compare the results.

Note: *Each compression method is explained at the end of the Imagcomp.pdf file.*

4 When you are done viewing the example file, choose File > Close.

Checking filenames

Adobe recommends that your filenames consist of one to eight characters (no spaces) optionally followed by an extension (a period and from one to three characters). Use .pdf as the file extension for your PDF documents. Most Web browsers,

Web servers, and versions of Microsoft Windows have been configured to associate .pdf files with Acrobat Exchange, Reader, or the Web browser plug-in and to launch the appropriate program when encountered.

Examining sample *Welcome* documents

When first opening a CD-ROM or visiting a Web site, it may be difficult for your users to determine where to start or to determine what's in the document collection. To point your users in the right direction, include a "welcome" PDF document, or on the Web or an intranet, you might want to use an HTML Web page as your welcome document.

Tip: On CD-ROMs you should also include a ReadMe text file that contains Acrobat Reader installation instructions and any necessary last-minute information about the CD-ROM.

Opening sample *Welcome* documents

Take a moment to look at some sample *Welcome* PDF documents. The one-page sample documents have been extracted from their document collections; therefore, the links on these pages are not functional.

1 Choose File > Open, locate and select Welcome.pdf in the Projectc folder, and click Open.

2 Click the preview images in the document window to view the different sample documents.

3 When you are finished viewing the samples, close the Welcome.pdf document.

Adding links to a *Welcome* document

We have created a *Welcome* document for you to use with your document collection contained in the PROJECTS folder. You will add some cross-document links from a *Welcome* document to some of the documents in the PROJECTS folder.

1 Choose File > Open, and locate and select Welcome2.pdf in the Projectc folder.

2 Save it in the PROJECTS folder.

3 Select the link tool and drag a link rectangle around the thumbnail representing Lesson 2.

4 For Appearance Type, choose Invisible Rectangle.

5 For Action Type, choose Go to View.

6 With the Create Link dialog box still open, choose File > Open, and locate and select 02work.pdf in the PROJECTS folder.

Note: If you did not save your documents in the PROJECTS folder, locate and select the lesson files from the individual lesson folders.

7 In the Create Link dialog box, choose a magnification level you are comfortable with, and click Set Link.

8 Follow steps 3–7 again for the Lesson 3 thumbnail. (The filename used for Lesson 3 was Flyer.pdf.)

9 Save Welcome2.pdf in the PROJECTS folder.

Adding Document Info data to PDF files

Document information screens provide users with basic information about a file and another way to index a file in a collection of documents. The Title, Subject, Author, and Keyword fields in the General Document Info dialog box can be entered and edited in Acrobat Exchange.

Looking at Document Info fields

Take a look at the information loaded in the Document Info fields for the Welcome2.pdf document.

1 If it is not already open, choose File > Open, locate and select Welcome2.pdf, and click Open.

2 Choose File > Document Info > General.

Notice that the entries in the Title, Subject, Author, and Keyword fields are empty and can be edited. The other entries represent file information generated by the PDF creator. Document Info fields should be filled in for each document. Many Web search engines use the Document Info field to display an item in their Search Results list. If you do not fill in the Document Info Title field, a nondescript file-name appears in the Search Results list.

Entering Document Info data

If you are going to index your document collection with Acrobat Catalog, it is a good idea to enter Document Info data for all your files. The Document Info field data provides another way to search for information in a document collection. See Lesson 11 for details.

In this lesson, you will enter Document Info information in only the Welcome2.pdf file, but it should be done for all files in a document collection.

1 Enter the following information:

• For Title, enter **Acrobat 3.0 Classroom in a Book.**

• For Subject, enter **Tutorials.**

• For Author, enter **your name.**

• For Keywords, enter **Acrobat, tutorials, lessons, help.**

2 Click OK.

3 Choose File > Save As. Replace the existing file, and close it.

Once you finish with entering Document Info in all the files in your document collection, you are ready to stage your documents, optimize them, and index them.

Organizing your staging area

If possible, you should set up your staging area on a network file server and keep a copy of the original files in another location. Backup copies can save you from having to recreate files if, by chance, they are mistakenly deleted or corrupted. For this project, you will use the PROJECTS folder as your staging area.

Organizing the documents in folders lends an intuitive organization and leads readers to the information they need. Before you publish your document collection, consider asking others to use the folder structure in your staging area to make sure your organization is easy to understand.

Optimizing PDF documents

Optimization involves consolidation and reordering of your PDF documents. Duplicate background objects (text, line art, and images) are consolidated to reduce the file size significantly, and objects in the PDF file format are reordered for *page-at-a-time downloading* over the Internet. With page-at-a-time downloading (byte-serving), the Web server sends only the requested page of information to the user, not the entire PDF document.

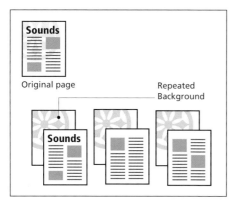

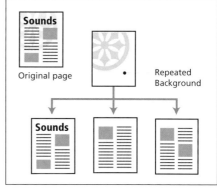

Not optimized   *Optimized*

You can optimize a file every time you choose the Save As command by selecting the Optimize option (selected by default), or you can Batch Optimize a collection of documents all at once. In this section, you will batch optimize the files in the PROJECTS folder all at once.

1 In Acrobat Exchange, choose File > Batch Optimize.

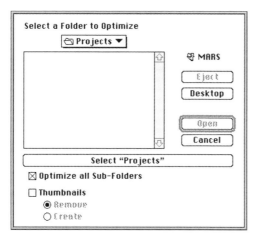

2 Do one of the following:

• In Windows, double-click to select the PROJECTS folder, and click OK.

• On the Macintosh, click to select the PROJECTS folder, and click Select "Projects".

An optimization status bar appears. Once optimization is complete, the status bar goes away and the files are almost ready for distribution.

Indexing your document collection

If you are publishing your documents on a CD-ROM, you should use Acrobat Catalog to index your document collection. The index created by Acrobat Catalog is not searchable over the World Wide Web or a company intranet. If you would like searching capabilities over the Web or your intranet, your PDF documents have to be indexed by a Web search engine that supports indexing PDF documents. See www.adobe.com/proindex/acrobat/websearch.html for a list of Web search engines that support PDF indexing.

You will now index the documents located in the PROJECTS folder.

1 Start Acrobat Catalog.

2 Choose Index > New (Windows) or File > New (Macintosh), and enter **Class Files** as the name of the index.

3 Enter the following information about the index in the Index Description box: **Completed files from Acrobat Classroom in a Book.**

4 Click the Add button in the Include Directories box, and do one of the following:

• In Windows, double-click to select the PROJECTS folder, and click OK.

• On the Macintosh, click to select the PROJECTS folder, and click Select "PROJECTS".

5 Click Build, and name it **Class.pdx.**

6 Open the PROJECTS folder, save the index inside that folder, and click OK (Windows) or Save (Macintosh).

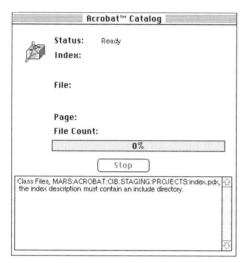

7 Exit (Windows) or Quit (Macintosh) Catalog after reading Index Build Successful in the Catalog message window.

Automatically loading an index

Before you search an index, that index needs to be loaded in the available index list. Normally you load an index manually. But you can associate an index with a file, so that whenever that file is opened, the associated index is automatically added to the available index list.

In this section, you will associate the class index with the Welcome2.pdf document, so that whenever the welcome document is opened the class index will automatically be available for searching.

1 Return to Acrobat Exchange.

2 Choose File > Open, locate and select Welcome2.pdf in the PROJECTS folder, and click Open.

3 Click the Search button in the toolbar, and click Index. Notice that the Class Files index is not listed as an available index.

4 Choose File > Document Info > Index.

5 On the Macintosh, click Choose Index and Browse.

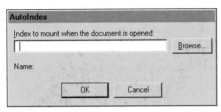 

Windows dialog box   *Macintosh dialog box*

6 Locate and select Class.pdx in the PROJECTS folder, and click Open and OK.

7 Choose File > Save. Save the file and close it.

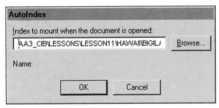 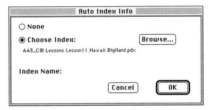

Windows dialog box   *Macintosh dialog box*

8 Choose File > Open. Reopen the Welcome2.pdf file.

9 Click the Search button in the toolbar, and click Indexes. Notice that the Class Files index is now listed as an available index. Click OK.

10 Enter **Adeline** in the Search for text containing box, and click Search.

Flyer.pdf appears in the Search Results list. This is an example of a nondescript file-name that can appear in a Search Results list. If we had entered a title in the Document Info Title field before indexing the file, that would have appeared in the list.

11 Open Flyer.pdf.

12 Choose File > Close.

It is important to maintain relative file relationships once you have completed making cross-document links and indexing your collection. If you alter a relative file relationship by moving a file to a folder it was not in when a link to it was created or after using Catalog to index the collection, linking and searching will produce error messages instead of link destinations and highlighted search terms.

Including Acrobat Reader installers

Don't forget to include Acrobat Reader installers on your CD-ROM or Web site. You can also point to the Reader installers on the Adobe Web site from your Web page. You should include a ReadMe text file at the top level of your CD-ROM that describes how to install Acrobat Reader and provides any last-minute information. If posting the installers on your Web site, include the Reader installation instructions with the link to the downloadable software.

Testing your document collection

Once you have staged your documents and the Acrobat Reader installers, test your document links, bookmarks, actions, forms, and indexes to ensure that everything works the way you planned.

Double-checking the checklist

You should double-check content, layout, artwork, and so forth of any document that you intend to distribute. As you have seen with this lesson, electronic documents add a few other items to your checklist. We have created a checklist to help you double-check the basics. Of course, feel free to add to the list to help you complete your own projects.

Checklist:

• Content complete

• Electronic enhancements, links and bookmarks, and so forth complete

• Document Info added to all files

• Filenames have one to eight characters plus a .pdf extension

• Files are organized appropriately

• Optimization is complete

• Files are indexed (CD-ROM distribution)

• Files tested in staging area

• Maintain file structure when delivering your document collection to your Web server administrator or CD-ROM creator

Review

Congratulations! You have just completed *Adobe Acrobat 3.0 Classroom in a Book*. You've learned quite a bit about using Acrobat to create, enhance, and publish your electronic documents. As you continue to work with Adobe Acrobat, you might want to refer to specific lessons in this book to remind yourself of particular procedures. Remember to check the Adobe Web site for the latest information about Adobe Acrobat and all the other great products and services available.

To test your knowledge of the concepts and techniques you learned in this project, answer the following questions:

• What compression methods remove data from an image? [Hint: Check the Imagcomp.pdf file.]

• What compression methods do not remove data from an image? [Hint: Check the Imagcomp.pdf file.]

• Why should you compress your images in a PDF file?

• Why is it recommended that you name your files with one to eight characters plus a .pdf extension?

• What does optimization do to your PDF files?

• Are you allowed to include the Acrobat Reader installers on CD-ROMs that you publish?

Q&A

Review Questions & Answers

Lesson 1

Q How do you return to a previous view of a PDF document?

A Click the Go Back button to return to a previous view. Click the Go Forward button to reverse the action of the Go Back button.

Q What kind of document information is displayed in the status bar?

A The status bar displays the total number of pages in the PDF document, the page number of the current page, the magnification of the view, the printed size of the page, and the page layout preference.

Q How do you navigate to a page using thumbnails?

A Click the image of a thumbnail to go to the corresponding page in the document.

Q What is the difference between the find tool and the Search command?

A The find tool looks for information in the current document. The Search command lets you look for information in a collection of documents by searching an index that has been created for the document collection by Acrobat Catalog.

Q What features are displayed in the overview window?

A Bookmarks and thumbnails appear in the overview window.

Q What key do you press to activate the zoom-out tool?

A To activate the zoom-out tool when the zoom tool is selected, press Ctrl (Windows) or Option (Macintosh).

Q How do you activate a movie clip?

A Select the hand tool and move the pointer into the document. When the pointer changes to the filmstrip icon, click to activate the movie clip. To stop the movie, press Esc.

Q How do you access the Acrobat online guides?

A Choose the desired guide from the Help menu (Windows) or the Balloon Help menu (Macintosh). The menu lists online guides for each component of Adobe Acrobat, as well as the *Acrobat Online Guide*, which contains a table of contents that leads you to the appropriate component guide.

Lesson 2

Q Name three ways in which you can switch to a different page.

A You can switch pages by clicking the Next Page or Previous Page buttons in the toolbar, by dragging the scroll box in the scroll bar, by clicking the page-number box in the status bar and entering a page number, by clicking a link or bookmark that jumps to a different page, or by clicking the thumbnail for a different page.

Q Name three ways in which you can change the view magnification.

A You can change the magnification by clicking the Actual Page, Fit Page, and Fit Width buttons in the toolbar, marquee-dragging with the zoom tool, clicking in the document with the zoom tool, pressing Ctrl (Windows) or Option (Macintosh) and clicking with the zoom tool to zoom out, choosing a preset magnification from the magnification box menu in the status bar, or clicking the magnification box and entering a specific percentage.

Q What kinds of destinations can a link jump to?

A A link can jump to a different view within the same or different PDF document or to a page on the World Wide Web. A link can also jump to other application files, and be used to trigger actions such as play sounds or execute a menu command.

Q How do you control the view magnification of a link destination?

A You can set the magnification of the destination view by choosing a preset level from the Magnification menu in the Create Link dialog box, or by choosing Fixed from the Magnification menu and adjusting the magnification of the destination page as desired.

Q How do you edit an existing link?

A To edit a link, select the link tool and double-click inside the link in the document to open the Link Properties dialog box. After you have changed the desired properties, click Set Link.

Lesson 3

Q Why should you use the Acrobat Distiller PPD when creating a PostScript file that will be processed by Acrobat Distiller?

A A PPD tells the printer driver what type of device you are printing to and what are the capabilities of that device. In the case of the Acrobat Distiller PPD, the PPD tells the driver to include information such as color and custom page size. If you create a file with color and a custom page size, but chose a PPD that does not let the driver know about those document properties, Distiller will output a black-and-white, 8-1/2-by-11 inch PDF file. So, it is always best to use the PPD for the device to which you are outputting the document.

Q If your documents contain placed EPS images, which PDF creator should you use to create a PDF file?

A If your documents contain placed EPS images and you want to retain the scalability of the image, you should use Acrobat Distiller to create a PDF file.

Q What are the advantages of using Distiller to create PDF files instead of PDF Writer?

A Distiller:

• Retains image resolution of placed EPS images.
• Provides precise control of image compression and downsampling
• Retains PostScript features such as OPI comments in PDF documents
• Provides batch processing options
• Can be shared across a network

Q What are the advantages of using PDF Writer to create PDF files instead of Distiller?

A PDF Writer:

• Maintains searchable text in documents created with embedded TrueType fonts from Windows 95 and Windows NT.
• Can be used in a Macro to create PDF documents.
• Can be faster to create a PDF document than Distiller.

Q Why is it important to enter information in the Document Info fields?

A It is important to enter Document Info because Document Info fields are used by search engines to help you categorize documents and provide a descriptive title for Search Results lists.

Q How would you create a PostScript file from your favorite application?

A Follow the instructions in the "Creating a PostScript file" on page 62 or follow the instructions in the application's or printer driver's user guide.

Q Why is there a one-step and a two-step method to creating PDF files with Distiller?

A The one-step method streamlines the process of creating PDF files with Distiller. The two-step method accommodates low-memory computers.

Lesson 4

Q How do print-on-demand electronic documents differ from documents optimized for online use?

A Print-on-demand documents tend to be longer, text-intensive documents that were originally designed for paper output. Optimized online documents have been redesigned for optimal display on a monitor and may contain more graphics and screen-based navigational features.

Q What hardware and software do you need to view PDF documents?

A You can view PDF documents on any type of computer or platform—Windows, Macintosh, UNIX, or OS/2. In addition to a computer, you need Acrobat Reader or Exchange to view PDF documents.

Q What kinds of media can you use to distribute PDF documents?

A You can distribute PDF documents via floppy disk, CD-ROM, electronic mail, corporate intranet, or the World Wide Web. You can also print PDF documents and distribute them as printed documents.

Q What factors determine the layout and appearance of an HTML page? A PDF page?

A In HTML, the layout of a document depends on the structural relationships between graphics and different text formats. The fonts are determined by the font settings of the Web browser. A PDF document is essentially an electronic snapshot of a source graphics or page layout file. The layout and appearance are determined by the application used to create the source file.

Q What kinds of typefaces and type sizes are best suited for on-screen display?

A Large typefaces with simple, clean shapes display most clearly on the screen. Sans serif fonts are more suitable than serif fonts, which contain embellishments more suitable for the printed page.

Lesson 5

Q What happens when you click the text of a bookmark? What happens when you click the page icon for a bookmark?

A Clicking the text of a bookmark links you to a view destination or activates the action that has been assigned to the bookmark. Clicking the page icon for a bookmark selects the bookmark for editing.

Q How do you change your viewed area or magnification using thumbnails?

A To adjust the area of view, drag the view box inside the thumbnail. To adjust the magnification, drag the lower right corner of the view box to resize it.

Q Name two ways in which you can enter an article thread.

A You can enter an article thread by choosing View > Articles, selecting the desired article, and clicking View, or by using the hand tool to click inside a section of an article. When the hand tool is positioned over an article, a downward pointing arrow with a bar above it appears inside the hand pointer.

Q Can you assign an action to a thumbnail?

A No, you cannot assign actions to thumbnails.

Q If you replace a page with links on it, what happens to the links after the replacement?

A Because links reside on a different layer from the content of a page, they are not affected when the page content is replaced. Your links will still jump to the correct destination or activate the correct action after the replacement.

Lesson 6

Q How can you automate the creation of links and bookmarks?

A To generate links and bookmarks automatically from a FrameMaker or PageMaker file, create and format cross-references and a table of contents in the original application. These features are automatically converted to links and bookmarks when the file is distilled.

Q How do you change the order of pages in a document?

A You change the page order by selecting the thumbnails corresponding to the pages you want to move and dragging the thumbnails to their new location.

Q What kinds of text attributes can you change from within Exchange?

A You can use the touch-up tool to change text formatting—font, size, color, and alignment—or to change the text itself. When changing the font, you can choose from the Base 13 fonts and any fonts that have been fully embedded in the document.

Q How do you select multiple thumbnails?

A To select more than one thumbnail, click the page-number box for the first thumbnail. Hold down Shift and click the page-number boxes for the other thumbnails to add them to the selection.

Q How do you insert an entire PDF file into another PDF file?

A To insert all the pages from a PDF file into another PDF file, choose Document > Insert Pages and select the file you wish to insert.

Q How do you insert one page or a range of pages from one PDF file into another?

A To insert a selection of pages from one PDF file into another, open both the files with their thumbnails visible. Select the thumbnails for the pages you wish to insert, and drag the thumbnails to the desired location in the overview window for the other document.

Q What types of actions can you assign to links and bookmarks?

A You can assign Execute Menu Item, Go To View, Import Form Data, Movie, Open File, Read Article, Reset Form, Show-Hide Field, Sound, Submit Form, World Wide Web link, and None actions to links and bookmarks.

Project: Creating an Online Version of a Book

Q How do you generate a PDF index automatically when distilling a FrameMaker file?

A To generate a PDF index automatically from a FrameMaker file, add index markers to the original file. Name the document filenames exactly as you want the final PDF filenames to appear, and create the book file. Generate the index and rename it in Windows Explorer or the Finder. Redirect the index path in the book file to the renamed index. Finally, print the book file to PostScript and enter an asterisk as the book filename to preserve the document filenames and create usable links.

Q What does Distiller's compression scheme do?

A Distiller's compression scheme compresses the text, line art, and bitmap images in a document to reduce file size.

Q What are the advantages of embedding fonts?

A When you embed the fonts in a PDF document, the document displays with its original fonts on any system, regardless of whether the fonts are installed on the system.

Q How can the table of contents for a printed publication differ from the table of contents for a strictly online publication?

A In a printed publication, a single table of contents at the front of the book lists the featured topics. In an optimized online publication, the table of contents is spread over a series of nested, hierarchical screens. The screen listing the main topics links to screens listing the subtopics, which in turn link to screens containing the topics themselves.

Q How do you insert a new article box into an existing article thread?

A Choose Tools > Article and click inside an existing article box to select it. Then click the plus sign that appears at the bottom of the box. Any new article boxes you draw will be inserted after this selected article box.

Q How do you end an article thread?

A To end an article thread, click End Article in the status bar.

Lesson 7

Q What kinds of actions can you assign as page actions?

A You can assign Execute Menu Item, Go To View, Import Form Data, Movie, Open File, Read Article, Reset Form, Show-Hide Field, Sound, Submit Form, World Wide Web link, and None actions to a page action.

Q When using the movie tool to add a movie to a document, why should you click instead of drag?

A If you drag with the movie tool, the movie is resized to fit inside the dragged area on the page, resulting in distorted image quality. Clicking with the movie tool lets you place a movie in its original size on the page.

Q What is a movie poster?

A A movie poster consists of a still image of the first movie frame. You can choose whether or not to display a movie poster in the activation area for a movie on the page.

Q Name three ways in which you can add sound to a PDF document?

A You can add sound to a PDF document as a page action, as an action associated with a link or a bookmark, and as a sound clip placed with the movie tool.

Q Can you edit the content of movie and sound clips from within Exchange?

A No.

Lesson 8

Q What file format must a graphic be saved in before you can use it as a button icon?

A To use a graphic as a button icon, the graphic must be in PDF format.

Q If your original button icon is 5 inches by 5 inches in your graphics program and the field you draw in a PDF file is 3 inches by 3 inches, what size will the button icon appear in the PDF file?

A The button icon will be 3 inches by 3 inches in the PDF file. The original icon is resized to fit the button field you draw.

Q What is a mouse behavior?

A Mouse behavior refers to the position of the mouse or mouse button in relation to the button field; this position determines when the specified button action occurs. You can specify an action to occur when the mouse button is released or depressed, or when the mouse enters or exits the button field.

Q How can you make a button quit Exchange or Reader?

A To make a button that quits Exchange or Reader, create a button and choose Execute Menu Item as the action type. In the Menu Selection dialog box, choose File > Exit (Windows) or File > Quit (Macintosh).

Q Can a link or bookmark show or hide a field?

A Yes, a link or bookmark can either show a field or hide a field. For example, you can create a link that hides a graphic. You'd probably then want to create another link that shows this graphic.

Q Which style gives the appearance of a button without using an icon?

A To create a button appearance without adding an icon, choose Beveled for Style under the Appearance tab.

Lesson 9

Q What is the difference between a check box and a radio button?

A You can select multiple check boxes, whereas you can select only one radio button out of a series.

Q What is the purpose of a Submit button?

A A Submit button sends form data from a Web-based form to a CGI application, which routes the information to a database.

Q When will a Submit button send data to a CGI application on a Web server?

A To send data with a Submit button, you must set up and run a CGI application on a Web server and assign a destination URL to the Submit button.

Q Which fields will populate in a form if you use the Import > Form Data command?

A When you import data from a form data file, the fields that share names in common with the imported data fields will be populated.

Q What is a combo box?

A A combo box consists of a pop-up list of items from which users can choose one item.

Q How do you copy a form field?

A To copy a form field, select the form tool and make sure all form fields are deselected. Hold down Ctrl (Windows) or Option (Macintosh) and drag the desired field to create and move a copy of the field.

Project: Multimedia Project

Q How do you create a button on page 6 with Go to View action that points at page 17?

A To create a button on page 6 that goes to page 17, do the following:

• Create the button on page 17.

• Choose Edit > Fields > Duplicate to duplicate the button to page 6.

• Optionally delete the button from page 17.

Q When selected, what does the Hidden option on the Appearance tab of the Field properties dialog box do?

A The Hidden option makes the field invisible until another action shows it.

Q What actions can you assign to a button?

A You can assign Execute Menu Item, Go To View, Import Form Data, Movie, Open File, Read Article, Reset Form, Show-Hide Field, Sound, Submit Form, World Wide Web link, and None actions to a button.

Q What other elements can you assign actions to?

A You can assign actions to links, bookmarks, page actions, and other types of form fields.

Q What happens to the display of a movie when you choose floating window as an option in your Movie Properties dialog box?

A The movie plays inside a floating window that appears in front of the document temporarily rather than on the document page.

Q Is there a way to display the menu bar or toolbar if they are hidden from view?

A Yes. To show the menu bar, press Ctrl+Shift+M (Windows) or Command+Shift+M (Macintosh). To show the toolbar, press Ctrl+Shift+B (Windows) or Command+Shift+B (Macintosh).

Lesson 10

Q How do you change the label and color of a note?

A To change the label and color of a note, choose File > Preferences > Notes, and change the desired settings.

Q What font is used in a note when viewed on your computer? On someone else's computer?

A When you view a note on your computer, the note displays the font that you have specified in the Note Preferences dialog box. When a different user views the note on their computer, they see the Note Preferences font that they have specified on their computer.

Q How do you create a file that contains only the labels, times, dates, and content of all notes added to a PDF file?

A Choose Tools > Summarize Notes.

Q What types of image files can you import into Exchange?

A You can import BMP, CompuServe GIF, PCX, or TIFF image files into Exchange.

Q What are the characteristics of a PDF Image file?

A In a PDF Image file, all the pictures and text are treated as images. You cannot edit the text using the touch-up tool or search the text using the find tool or Search command.

Q What is a "suspect" word?

A A suspect is a word that has probably been recognized incorrectly by the Capture plug-in. Capture provides its best guess for the characters in the suspect word and lets you correct its mistakes.

Q What types of security passwords can you assign to a document?

A You can assign a password that lets users open the document and one that lets users change the security options for the document.

Lesson 11

Q How can you distinguish an index file from a PDF file?

A An index file is identified by the PDX file extension that follows the filename.

Q What does the Search Results list display?

A The Search Results list displays the names of the documents that contain the search word or words. The documents are ranked according to the frequency of occurrence of the search items.

Q How does the Word Stemming option expand your search results?

A The Word Stemming option expands the search to look for words that contain the same root as the search word.

Q What key do you press to do a refined search?

A To change the Search button to Refine, press Ctrl (Windows) or Option (Macintosh).

Q Why should you enter Document Info field information in all your PDF documents?

A Entering Document Info field information for your documents lets you use Document Info fields to narrow down your search in an efficient manner.

Q Give two examples of Boolean expressions and what they do.

A One type of Boolean expression uses the OR operator to search for any of two or more search items. For example, "biking or skating" searches for documents that contain occurrences of either "biking" or "skating." Another Boolean expression uses the AND operator to search for occurrences of two or more search items in the same document. For example, "biking and skating" searches for documents that contain both "biking" and "skating."

Project: Distributing PDF documents

Q What compression methods remove data from an image?

A LZW 4-bit, LZW 8-bit, ZIP 4-bit, ZIP 8-bit, and JPEG compression levels are lossy, meaning data is removed from an image.

Q What compression methods do not remove data from an image?

A LZW, ZIP, CCITT, and Run length are lossless compression methods, meaning no data is removed from an image.

Q Why should you compress your images in a PDF file?

A You can reduce the file size of PDF documents and decrease the time to display pages by using Acrobat Distiller or PDF Writer to compress text, line art, and high-resolution bitmap images in the document.

Q Why is it recommended that you name your files with one to eight characters plus a .pdf extension?

A Adobe recommends that you name your files with one to eight characters plus a .pdf extension to ensure that file names do not get truncated and cause unexpected results on some platforms.

Q What does optimization do to your PDF files?

A Optimization involves consolidation and reordering of your PDF documents. Duplicate background objects (text, line art, and images) are consolidated to reduce the file size significantly and objects in the PDF file format are reordered for *page-at-a-time downloading* over the Internet. With page-at-a-time downloading (byte-serving), the Web server sends only the requested page of information to the user, not the entire PDF document.

Q Are you allowed to include the Acrobat Reader installers on CD-ROMs that you publish?

A Yes.

Index

A

Acrobat Catalog 11, 250–254, 282–283

Acrobat Distiller 11, 54–55, 61–62
   installing PPD 63–65
   setting compression 270
   specifying job options 138–141

Acrobat Exchange 10

Acrobat Online Guide 6

Acrobat Reader 10, 79, 80, 285

actions
   bookmark actions 132
   button actions 182–183, 220–221
   link actions 169–170, 171–172
   page actions 163–164

Actual Page button 20

Actual Size button 36

Adobe PageMaker 67

articles
   creating 149–151
   generating automatically 115
   setting magnification 151–152
   viewing 105–109, 153

B

bookmarks
   creating 89–90, 92
   displaying 18
   following 19, 89
   generating automatically 115
   moving 91
   nesting 95–96
   playing sounds 132
   selecting 91, 95
   setting actions 94–95
   setting destinations 93–94

Bookmarks and Page button 18

Boolean expressions 262–263

buttons
   assigning actions 182–183, 220–221, 223–226
   assigning icons 181–182
   creating 179–183
   duplicating 184
   editing 187
   linking to World Wide Web 190–192
   mouse behaviors 182–183
   moving 183
   resizing 183, 220
   selecting 183
   showing or hiding a field 189–190

C

Capture Online Guide. See Acrobat Online Guide

Capture plug-in 11

capturing images 240

Catalog Online Guide. See Acrobat Online Guide

Catalog. *See* Acrobat Catalog

compressing files 139, 269–271, 273–274

creating PDF
   from Adobe PageMaker 67–71
   with Acrobat Distiller 59–60
   with PDF Writer 56–58

cropping pages 118–119, 241

D

Distiller Online Guide. See Acrobat Online Guide

Distiller. *See* Acrobat Distiller

Document Info
   entering 280

searching with 260
   viewing 279

downsampling 139–140

E

Exchange Online Guide. See Acrobat Online Guide

Exchange. *See* Acrobat Exchange

exporting
   form data 199
   notes 238

extracting pages 125

F

file security 243–245

filenames 275–276

find tool 21–22

First Page button 14

Fit Page button 14, 37

Fit Width button 36

fonts
   embedding 140–141
   installing 5

form tool 178, 203

forms
   buttons. *See* buttons
   check boxes 205–206
   combo boxes 206–208
   creating 202–210
   duplicating fields 209–210
   exporting data 199
   filling out 23–24, 198–199
   importing data 200–201
   moving fields 210
   radio buttons 208–210
   resetting 211–212
   submitting 202, 210–211

text fields 202–204

Full Screen mode 77, 131, 193

G

Go Back button 17

Go Forward button 18

H

hand tool 33

HTML format 79

I

Import plug-in 11

importing

form data 200–201

images 116, 240

notes 237

indexes

creating 250–254, 282–283

generating automatically 143–144

loading automatically 283–284

searching 254–256

selecting 255–256

inserting

article boxes 153–154

pages 122–124

L

Last Page button 14

link tool 39

links

creating 39–41

cross-document links 102–103

editing 41–45

executing menu
commands 129–131

following 16–17, 38–39

generating automatically 115

playing movies 169–170

playing sounds 171–172

setting actions 40, 169–170,
171–172

setting highlight 103

M

magnifying

with status bar 37

with thumbnails 99–100

with toolbar 36

with zoom tool 14–16, 37–38

monitor resolution 31–32

movie tool 162, 166–167

movies

adding with movie tool 166–169,
226–227

as link actions 169–170

as page actions 227

controller bar 168, 169

editing properties 170

floating windows 166

movie posters 168–169

playing 20, 166

system requirements 3

using with PDF 162

moving

bookmarks 91

pages 119–122

N

navigating

with hand tool 33

with scroll bar 36

with status bar 35, 37

with thumbnails 99

with toolbar 14

Next Page button 14

notes

creating 238

deleting 238

exporting 238

finding 20

formatting 238

importing 237

moving 237

opening 21

reading 237

summarizing 238

notes tool 238

numbering pages 125–126

O

optimizing files 280–282

overview window 13

closing 19

opening 18, 19

resizing 18, 89

P

page actions

assigning 163–164

playing 163

page layout 34–35

Page Only button 19

PDF 1, 10, 79–80

PDF Writer 11, 54–55, 61–62

Portable Document Format. *See* PDF

PostScript files

converting to PDF 59–60

creating 59, 65–67

PostScript language 10

PostScript printer driver 62

preferences

Full Screen 77

Max "Fit Visible" Magnification
151–152

Notes 238

opening document display
192–193, 228

Search 261

Weblink 47

Previous Page button 14

R

Reader. *See* Acrobat Reader
replacing pages 103–105
rotating pages 117

S

Scan plug-in 11
Search button *See* Search command
Search command 21, 254–256
   refining 259
   searching with Boolean
      expressions 262–263
   searching with Document Info 260
   selecting indexes 255–256
   setting options 256, 260
Search Next button 261
Search Previous button 261
search results
   ranking 257–258
   refining 259
   viewing 258–259
search tool. *See* Search command
select-text tool 90
Show-Hide Field actions
   activating 188
   assigning 188–190
sound
   as page actions 163–164
sounds
   as link actions 171–172
   playing 170–171
   system requirements 3
   using with PDF 162
status bar 13
suspects
   correcting 242–243
   displaying 242

T

text
   editing 126–127, 129
   formatting 127–129
   selecting 90, 128
thumbnails
   creating 97–98
   displaying 19
   inserting pages 122–123
   magnifying pages 99–100
   moving pages 119–122
   navigating with 19
   selecting 120
   view box 99–102
Thumbnails and Page button 19
touch-up tool
   editing text 126–127, 129
   selecting text 128

W

World Wide Web site
   linking to 45–47, 190–192
   searching 263
   submitting forms 202, 210–211
   using PDF with 79–80

Z

zoom tool 14–16, 37–38